'PoW to Lancashire Farmer!'

The remarkable life of Alec Barker

As told to and written by Anne Bonney

HELM
PRESS

Dedicated to my dear wife Norah and family

Published by Helm Press
10 Abbey Gardens, Natland, Kendal, Cumbria LA9 7SP
Tel: 015395 61321
E.mail: **helmpress@ktdbroadband.com**

First published 2005

Typeset in Berkley Old Style

ISBN 0 9550823 2 3

Typeset and printed by Stramongate Press, Kendal

Front cover: Alec demonstrating his crystal set

Back cover: PoWs in Alec's hut and pre-printed card Alec sent home

Contents

Alec in his garden.

Introduction

This is the life story of Alec Barker who was born in 1918, as told to me. Alec has had a full and wonderful life though his years as a PoW (Prisoner of War) in the Second World War in Silesia, between Poland and Germany, stand out as an important part in his memory.

These are the memories that he has of those times. Alec is coming up to his 88th year and we are commemorating at this time sixty years since the end of hostilities. So where hard facts and details of the history of the war are required we should turn to the prolific amount of excellent books written on the subject.

He recounts his later years, of marriage, farming and his loving family and it is they that we must thank for encouraging Alec to tell us his life story. During the past few years they have wanted him to write it down, and this is what we have now done.

Special thanks to Margaret Hemsworth for lending information belonging to her late husband George concerning 'The March' the PoWs were forced to go on. Thanks also to Tony Chaloner (Alec's nephew) and other relations and friends that have helped in any way.

So forgive any mistakes that may have been made in the telling – it is Alec's life story as he remembers it. Please read on and enjoy this remarkable life as only Alec could have told it.

Anne Bonney

Anne Bonney
October 2005

Family wedding Terrace Hall 1918

Front row (l to r) Owen Barker; (grandmother) Jemima Halls (nee Bacon); groom - RAF pilot's uniform – William Henry Stow (Gt. Horkesley); bride – Elsie Halls; little girl member of groom's family and Hilda Barker.

Middle row: ? ; ? ; ? ; Montague Barleyman (married Emma Halls).

2

Chapter One

Family Background

I was born Alec Edward Barker on the 15th September 1918, in Colchester, Essex and was the youngest of three children. The eldest was my sister Hilda Constance, born on the 25th October, 1900 and then Owen Percy my brother, born in 1904. My father, Percy Barker, was born in 1878 at Little Bentley, near Colchester and married my mother, Kate Halls, in February 1900 at her home. My mother was born at Terrace Hall, Great Horkesley, near Colchester in 1882 to Henry and Esther Jemima Halls. My father had been given Brook Farm, at Little Bentley, a two hundred and fifty acre arable farm (maybe rented), by my grandfather, Albert Peter Barker, when he was eighteen. My grandfather had farmed at Great Bentley Hall where the village green is said to be one of the largest in the country. During the First World War horses and soldiers were billeted on the farm. My father farmed there until 1921 when he sold off his farm and let all his farmland out.

My father then moved from the Tendring Hundred area (Colchester to the sea) up to Ipswich, where he bought Stoke Park, a large estate, on the 29th September of that year, with the intention of developing it. He did develop some of the estate into building land and moved into the large mansion, which had twenty-one bedrooms which were described in the sale particulars as large and lofty bedchambers! Fortunately there was heating by a coal boiler. Stoke Park Estate was in the Parish of St. Mary Stoke, and within the Borough of Ipswich, only one mile from the main line station on the Great Eastern Railway. There was a Round Lodge guarding the broad carriage drive leading to the mansion, pleasure grounds, lodge and 62 acres of Home Farm, cottage and 82 acres, six small holdings with areas of 2 to 21 acres, 14 blocks of accommodation land with areas of 2 to 32 acres, 14 capital residential sites fronting Belstead and Wherstead Road and Birkfield Lane with areas of 2 to 9 acres and beautifully timbered grounds having magnificent views of the River Orwell. The mansion was substantially built with white Suffolk brick, with slated and leaden roofs, the elevations being partly faced with stone, and had on the eastern front a lofty veranda or Piazza supported by nine stone pillars and on the south a spacious front entrance court, enclosed by a dwarf stone wall, on which was the stone-built Porte Cochere.

Father had two maidservants (there were nine servants' bedrooms and a housemaid's Room) in the house, two gardeners for the large garden and two farmhands. We brought old Ted Watson, the gardener, and Albert

Taylor, the farmhand, with us from Bentley. Meanwhile mother and the rest of us moved into Broughton Lodge, a big house which father had rented in Ipswich until we could move in to Stoke Park. Mother was a bit taken aback with the size of the place, it was massive, with countless rooms as she had it all to carpet, curtain and fit out comfortably for us all to live in. Father took down a wing of the house and the money from selling the lead paid for the refurbishment.

There was a wonderful, big walled garden, cold frames, greenhouses and potting sheds. The gardeners did a good job keeping the lovely box hedges that surrounded the well laid out beds. We also had asparagus beds, soft fruits, and a glasshouse containing an orangery. It was kept hot in the old days but I don't think we kept it up. The kitchen garden was kept, as father was keen on that, likewise the mansion.

There was one cottage for one of the farmhands and another cottage for one of the gardeners. The others lived nearby and travelled in daily. One of the gardeners used to drive the car we had, as father never drove. He had a French car, the De Dion Bouton. I remember father telling me about the incident when the gardener/chauffeur went down to Ipswich to collect his new French car from Botwoods. They gave him an hour's tuition on how to drive a car. He gingerly started the engine, put it into gear, put his foot down on the accelerator and promptly shot through the plate glass window. Obviously the hour's tuition was not enough!

I used to like playing with the gardener's children and I remember we used to pretend to smoke dry nettle stalks, play hide and seek, cricket and all the other usual games, along with bird nesting and helping to make bonfires to get rid of garden refuse and other rubbish.

Hilda, my sister had a boyfriend at this time and he used to let me sit on his knee and steer the Morris Cowley ('Bullnose') car when he was driving (in the grounds) – it was great fun and nice having somebody else young about the place.

Father tried to develop one part of the park for building land but was unable to, as the Great Eastern Railway passed over at that point on a very low bridge and, of course, they would not allow any development within that park area. My father got over this by selling this piece of land to William Paul of Paul's of Ipswich, who were large corn millers (still with BOCM). They generously donated this as a gift to the people of Ipswich and made it into a public park for everybody to enjoy. It is called Belstead Park and was opened by the then Duke of Gloucester.

The rest of the land my father sold off in different lots. The big house he sold to his tailor in Ipswich who had made his suits for twenty years. It was later demolished and only the gatehouse remains today. The rest of the area is now a large housing estate.

To begin with I attended a small school in the middle of Ipswich and had quite a long journey to it. I used to walk down the path from the house, through the large park and under the railway bridge to the road and there caught the Shotley bus for the short distance to school. Other times I walked to the station and caught the electric trackless trolley (solid rubber wheels but used the aerial track wires) bus up to Corn Hill (Corn Market) and then walked the short distance to school.

Percy Barker (father)
taken in South Africa in 1935.

Kate Barker (mother)

Chapter Two

Cattle Dealing

My father was also a cattle dealer and bought Shorthorn bullocks twelve to eighteen months old. He would bring the cattle down from the north of England to where they were required in the south. He continued doing this as a sideline, utilising the land and farm buildings at Stoke Park and at the same time knew he would be able to develop this and make a lot of money. At that time the country was in a slump and nobody had much money. He was a shrewd businessman and that is how he got established.

He had started travelling up to the north of England in the early 1900s, visiting farms in North Lancashire, Cumberland and Westmorland. He travelled by train to the stations ie. Carnforth, Lancaster, Barbon, Bay Horse. Then the following week he would travel further up north to Appleby and Lazonby, as well as out to West Cumbria, to the coastal market towns. He took time to get to know the people who lived in the area and then he would get a local man to act as his agent. They perhaps had the local pub and they would know the farms and where the local farmers lived who kept Shorthorns. These agents would then meet him at the station and he would stay at their hotel, pub or private house. Then they would take him round in a two-wheeled horse and trap to the various farms that had Shorthorn cattle.

A successful deal would be made by the 'knock of the hand'. How much? £6? 'No, I will give you £4!' They would haggle away until a fair price was agreed! The deal would be complete. Three agents that acted for him were a Mr Parker from Casterton; Mr Postlethwaite at the Bay Horse; and William Lowis, a semi-retired farmer from Shap. He always stayed at 'The Greyhound' at Shap and used to comment on how cold it was.

After the deal was struck, the farmers on the fell farms were required to walk the cattle in twos and threes, with sometimes a halter on the odd calf, along to the nearest railway station and there they would be loaded into cattle trucks for transportation down to Ipswich and the eastern counties. The farmers then received their cheques and the deal would be complete. Honesty always existed in those days with farmers 'their word was their bond' and so was his.

When the cattle reached Ipswich they would go either to his or his friends' farms. He would then sell them on from there or send them out to customers. He used Home Farm at Stoke Park as a holding farm. People would come and purchase what they wanted and any left would go to store markets at Ipswich or Norwich. These cattle were then fattened in the yards (sheds) and were very good beef. Father would sometimes buy them back and send them to the butchers down at Southampton where the big ocean liner companies would buy them for their passengers. In the early days, of course, the muck and straw was a valuable fertiliser for the East Anglian farms, as there were no artificial fertilisers as such then.

After a time he decided the travelling was too great. He was travelling north by train on Tuesday night and then coming back on the Friday night every week. He didn't like this as it meant being away from home too long and decided to move north.

So we moved up to Lancaster in 1928/9 and through Estate Agents – Procter & Birkbeck, rented Scotforth House. This was a large house which father rented for £52 a year. There was no garage and father wanted one, so the owner agreed to build one. I was only a young school child at the time but remember watching these stonemasons working away. The garden covered an acre and a half and we lived there until 1930 when we moved to Glenholme on a private road just off Westbourne Road, as father wanted to be near Castle Station for his business.

Chapter Three

School

I now attended the Friends School, which was next to the Quaker Meeting House, down by Castle Station, in Lancaster. There were two railway stations in Lancaster then, the other being Green Ayre. I was living at home and attending school, my brother and sister, of course, were much older than me and had both moved away by this time. My parents were rather elderly, my mother was forty-three when I was born. So it was decided that it would be a good thing for me to go away to boarding school.

I was sent to Hutton Grammar School, near Preston. The headmaster was a Major in the First World War – Reverend C. P. Hinds. There were only fifty boarders. It was a hard but good school. There were bare boards, rough food and cold dormitories. I lived in the schoolhouse and the headmaster's wife, Mrs Hinds, did the catering. She tried to make as much money as possible - hence we got very bad food. I was allowed to take a tuck box to school and one of the things I took with me was a bottle of Heinz Tomato Ketchup – this was to enable me to get that awful food down.

School was very tough in those days and you never left it except during holidays. There was a tuck shop in the school grounds where we could purchase strong mints, acid drops, toffees and ice cream. I don't think they sold any food, if they did we would all have been buying it to supplement those awful meals. The little old man who had the shop across the road ran it but we were not allowed to cross the road to his shop, as that was out of bounds.

However, we were allowed out at half term and I used to go and stay with Hilda, who was now married (1930) and living in a nice house at St. Anne's, near Blackpool. She had met Charles Chaloner when she was living with us in Scotforth. Charles was a wholesale chemist and was living in Preston where he had his depot. His business covered quite a large area of Lancashire travelling to chemist shops in towns and villages around Lancaster, Morecambe, Preston and Chorley. I looked forward to my visits, enjoying the nice meals and freedom during the periods of time I stayed with them.

At school I was keen on sport, arithmetic and languages. We had a German master who taught German and I liked French. We also took physics and chemistry and I enjoyed the practical side. I also took a commercial course and was taught typing and shorthand. We attended church twice on a

Friends School, Lancaster, May 1930.
Front row (l to r) John Bee; Harry Kinloch; Lesley Bell (Grocers shops, Lancaster);.
2nd row (l to r) ? Melling; ? Gardner; ? : ? Riley; ? Young; wearing glasses – Mr Watson, Mrs Watson and Mr Nesbett.
Back row (l to r) 4th boy – Alec; ? ; Dennis Jackson (Yates & Jackson – public house); ? ; Kenneth Dowbiggen.

10

Sunday. I did well at school and obtained my school certificate.

My brother left Ipswich in 1922 and became a stockbroker on the floor of the London Stock Exchange and remained so until he died in his early seventies. He worked for Vandervelt and Keil and then Rogersons. He lived in London and after I left school I used to go and stay with him and we had some good times. I, of course, had led a rather sheltered life at boarding school and at home with my elderly parents. I thought my brother had quite a good life. He was a bachelor at the time and had a flat just off Oxford Street which was within walking distance of the Oxford and Bond Street Underground Stations. He had a live-in French girlfriend at the time and she used to take me out sightseeing during the day to places like the Science Museum, Madame Tussard's and the Houses of Parliament.

At night we went to nightclubs, Soho and to Café Anglais. We dined at the Hungarian Restaurant and 'Genero', the Italian Restaurant in Soho. We also went to the Windmill Theatre, which was open all day, and the London Palladium where the Crazy Gang, Nervo and Knox, Flannigan and Allen, Norton and Gold would sometimes be performing. I was beginning to get a taste for life and what it was all about. I always wore a suit and at night a bow tie and tails, certainly at proper balls – you would wear a white shirt and white bow tie. I finished this all off with a dark Crombie overcoat. The girls wore long evening gowns and capes. You never went to a dance unless you were in evening dress – anything else would have been unthinkable!

Outside the New Inn, at Yealand in 1937. Norah with her pet dog, Barbara her sister second on right and Mrs May Wilkinson their mother in front with friends.

Alec's Austin 10 Sports car parked outside the Bradford Arms in Morecambe.

Chapter Four

Working for Father

On leaving school at seventeen I joined father in his dealing business. I was getting on very well, travelling down to Ipswich for him and helping to sell his cattle there. We would attend various auction marts during the week: Harrison and Hetherington, Botchergate, Carlisle on the Wednesday, which was a store market, (now of course the new market is at Rosehill just off the M6), Hope's Auction at Wigton on a Thursday and Kidd's Auction Mart at Penrith on a Friday. Penrith also has new premises on the edge of town just off the motorway.

These sales went from the September until the last sale at Kirkby Stephen in November and that was the Luke Fair. This was an important and popular autumn sale that only sold bullocks (castrated males) one day and heifers (females) the next. Father loved this auction and attended every one, buying as many as two hundred and fifty cattle in one day which, of course, were all sent down to Ipswich. Store sales are solely where bullocks or heifers are bought and sold for fattening purposes.

My father had a good name for doing honest deals with people which were mainly done, as mentioned, by the shake of the hand. At auction marts, like everybody else, he would pay for them at the time. There was of course the 'luck penny'! This is when the seller would give a pound or so back to the purchaser for luck! My father was aptly known as the 'Bullock Man'!

I met Norah, who was later to become my wife, as a young girl when we were at school and she was attending Lancaster Girls' Grammar School. Her father, Tom Wilkinson, had a butcher's shop in Market Street, Lancaster. Norah had just the one sister, Barbara and lived at home with her parents. My mother played bridge with Mrs Wilkinson and we used to meet sometimes when we were collecting our mothers in those very early days. We were all quite friendly and that is how we started going out together.

Alec in army uniform.

Kenneth Dowbiggen (standing at front) at Trawsfnydd.

Chapter Five

Joining the Territorials – WW2

My father suggested to me, at this time, that we might rent a small farm and start farming. We would still continue dealing, of course, just like the old days. He had the opportunity of renting a farm from a Mr Oversby in the Melling area of Lancashire, near Carnforth.

War clouds were beginning to gather on the horizon and myself and some other like minded young lads whom I knew in Lancaster, could see that trouble was on the way and being patriotic, we discussed what we ought to do for our King and country. So in the spring of 1938 when I was out in Lancaster, I went along to the Recruiting Centre, which was at the Drill Hall in Dallas Road, (now gone and the land has been developed) saw the Recruiting Officer, signed the papers and joined up for two shillings (10p) a day as a Territorial (volunteer) in the 88th Field Regiment Royal Artillery – Battery 352. In the event of hostilities breaking out between Britain and Germany the Territorials would be the first to be called to the colours. Afterwards I went home and told my parents that I didn't need a farm anymore and that I would much rather 'do my bit for the country'!

In the course of that year and the following year we met twice a week for evening manoeuvres in the Quernmore area but we hadn't any proper guns or anything like that. Although in August 1938 we went to a firing camp at

Gun emplacement during training at the Firing Camp at Trawsfnydd.

DETAIL OF PERSONAL SIZED GARMENTS.

ARTICLE.	SIZE No.
Anklets, Web	
Blouse, B.D., or Jackets, K.D. or S.D.	
Boots, ankle	
Cap, Bonnet or Helmet	
Drawers, cellular or woollen	
Gloves, knitted	
Greatcoat	
Jersey, pullover	
Overalls	
Shirts	
Shoes, canvas	
Socks, worsted	
Trousers, B.D., S.D. or Shorts, K.D.	
Vests, woollen	

ALL RANKS

REMEMBER—Never discuss military, naval or air matters in public or with any stranger, no matter to what nationality he or she may belong.

The enemy wants information about you, your unit, your destination. He will do his utmost to discover it.

Keep him in the dark. Gossip on military subjects is highly dangerous to the country, whereas secrecy leads to success.

BE ON YOUR GUARD and report any suspicious individual.

Army Book 64 (Part I).

Soldier's Service Book

(Soldier's Pay Book, Army Book 64 (Part II) will be issued for active service.)

Entries in this book (other than those connected with the making of a Soldier's Will) are to be made under the superintendence of an Officer.

Instructions to Soldier.

1. You are held **personally responsible** for the safe custody of this book.

2. You will **always carry this book** on your person.

3. You must produce the book whenever called upon to do so by the Civil Police or by a competent military authority, viz., Officer, Warrant Officer, N.C.O. or Military Policeman.

4. You must not alter or make any entry in this book (except as regards your Will on pages 15 to 20).

5. Should you lose the book, you will report the matter to your immediate military superior.

6. On your transfer to the Army Reserve this book will be handed into your Orderly Room for transmission, through the O. i/c Records, to place of rejoining on mobilization.

7. You will be permitted to retain this book after discharge, but should you lose the book after discharge it cannot be replaced.

8. If you are discharged from the Army Reserve, this book will be forwarded to you by the O. i/c Records.

2

(1) SOLDIER'S NAME and DESCRIPTION on ATTESTATION.

Army Number _894992_

Surname (in capitals) _BARKER_

Christian Names (in full) _Alec Edward_

Date of Birth _15-9-18_

Trade on Enlistment _Live Stock Agent_ _Farmer_

Religious Denomination _C of E_

Approved Society _____

Membership No. _____

Enlisted at _Lancaster_ On _20.4.39_

For the :—
* Regular Army.   * Supplementary Reserve.
* Territorial Army.   * Army Reserve Section D.
    * Strike out those inapplicable.

For _____ years with the Colours and _____ years in the Reserve.

Signature of Soldier _____

Date _____

3

DESCRIPTION ON ENLISTMENT.

Height _5_ ft. _11½_ ins. Weight _153_ lbs.

Maximum Chest _40_ ins. Complexion _Fresh_

Eyes _Blue_   Hair _Brown_

Distinctive Marks and Minor Defects _____

_at 25c.   O/S 4/335_
_to 2/9/44._

CONDITION ON TRANSFER TO RESERVE:

Found fit for _____

Defects or History of past illness which should be enquired into if called up for Service _____

Date _____ 19 __

Initials of M.O. i/c _____

Alec's Soldier's Service and Pay Book

16

Trawsfnydd, Gwynedd, in Wales for a fortnight under canvas. We slept in round tents, twelve men per tent with our feet to the central pole. I had an Austin 10 open sports car and four of us used to make frequent visits to Llandudno and Colwyn Bay.

On 1st September, 1939 I was called up to attend the Drill Hall and issued with full uniform and battle kit. My army number was 894992 as a gunner (driver-in-charge). There were no rifles available, so we were given pick handles. Our 18-pounder artillery guns were replaced with 25-pounders. I went to Church Parade at the Priory Church, in Lancaster on Sunday 3rd September and the vicar disappeared into the vestry. At 11 am during the course of the service he came out and announced in a very sombre voice, 'We are at war with Germany!' That was the beginning of hostilities. Poland had been invaded and we had given Germany an ultimatum.

For the next three weeks we continued being kitted out, with other Territorials from Lancaster, Morecambe, Preston, Blackpool and a few regulars who joined us, one being George Hemsworth from Leeds, who became a good friend from that day until the day he died a few years ago. We were busy at this time collecting vehicles and mobilising, preparing to go to an as yet unknown destination. We had our injections etc and were still residing at home.

Then on 23rd September at 3 pm we assembled at the Drill Hall, we were all there in our vehicles. My troop was E' Troop and my job was driving the wireless truck, a Morris eight hundred weight. We had four guns and a maintenance truck. We assembled there in front of our commander, Major Gregson and in a strong rallying voice he said, 'You are now going to war and if necessary you will fight in your vehicles and die in them!'

With those momentous words ringing in our ears and without further ado we moved off. Our first stop that night was at Fulwood Barracks and we were informed that we would be sleeping in our vehicles. We still did not know where we were going. I managed to ring Norah and say where we were and that I had leave for that evening. She came through with a friend and met me at the Black Bull public house in Fulwood. We spent a nice evening together. I went back to the barracks to spend the night in the wireless vehicle. There was a touch of frost so it was very cold!

We set off in the morning to Prees Heath. Then from there we went to Hereford and sampled some cider that night. I used the water from the vehicle radiator to shave in the mornings. After four days travelling we eventually arrived at Newport, Monmouthshire. We parked our vehicles on

Promotions, Reductions, Appointments,   and Alterations in Allotment.

Pay (normal or tradesmen's rates).	RATES OF			TOTAL	Deduct Allotment or Compulsory Stoppage.	Net Rate to be Issued.		Date from which NET RATE OF PAY is issuable.	*Reason for changes in Net Rate (e.g., Promotions, Reductions, Alterations in Allotments, &c.).	Officer's Signature, Station and Date.
	Proficiency Pay.	Educational Proficiency Pay.	Military Proficiency Pay.			Figures	Words.			
2/-				2/-		2/-	Two Shillings	On Mob.		J.A. Cook Lincoln 25/9/39
2/-	6ᵈ	-	-	2/6	-	2/6	Two Shillings and Pence	3-3-40	Granted W.T.T. Part II order 25 d/ 3-4-40	S. Richards In the field 30 APR 1940

Particulars of Working and Additional Pay should be shown on page 8, not on pages 4 to 9.

* In addition to the above record, the Officer making the entry will write across the column for cash payments the nature of the casualty and the amended net rate of pay. He will also record in the same places all sentences of imprisonment and special stoppages, attesting such entries by his signature

---

Signature of Soldier _A R Barker._

Book opens on __2 2 DEC 1939__ 19 . (For the Net Daily Rate of pay see pages 4 to 9, and Notes thereon).

If the soldier was in debt on the above date, the amount to be recovered from the next pay due to him should be stated.

Debt £ _____ s _____

R.R.Hunter 2/Lt RA _____ O. C. Company, &c.

Cash Payments.

Date.	Place (If on active Service enter "Field.")	Amount. (State Currency.)	Signature and Unit of Officer.
2 2 DEC 1939	Field	2,000	R.R.Hunter 2/Lt RA
40	Field	520 —	A.R.W.Bee 2/Lt R.A
			1 2 JAN 1940
9.2.40	Fd.	200 Frs	S. Richards 2/Lt P.A
16-2-40	Fd	125 Frs	Lt Richards 2/Lt RA
28 FEB	Fd	100 Frs	S. Richards 2/Lt RA
1 MAR	Fd	150 Frs	R.R.Hunter 2/Lt RA
8 MAR	Fd	100 Frs	R. Bradley 2/Lt, RA
1 5 MAR 1940	Fd	100 Frs	S. Matthews B.S.M
2 2 MAR	Fd	150 Frs	S. Matthews B.S.M
Total Cash Payments to date ...		3745	

When a soldier is granted leave to England, an entry stating period of furlough is to be made in second column (i.e., "Place" column).

Soldier' Pay Book

18

the public park awaiting our vehicles and guns to be loaded onto the 'Maid of Man', one of the Isle of Man Steam Packet boats.

After two days loading, we were ready to set sail and slept on the deck, feeding on 'iron rations' of 'bully beef' (corn beef), biscuits and char (tea). This was the only food we had for two days before we docked at Nantes, on the River Loire, on the Brittany coast of France.

We disembarked that night, it was raining hard and we were marched through the streets and it took us some time to find the billets that had been allocated to us. When we found them it turned out to be an empty garage with a concrete floor. We only had one blanket each, the battledress we were wearing, together with overcoat and we just slept on that cold, hard, unforgiving floor. The next day we went down to the dock and collected our vehicles and equipment and then assembled on the racecourse in Nantes. The French soldiers we met were not very friendly and it didn't help Anglo-French relations when a British soldier was found dead in the river, believed murdered! Not a good start!

The following day we moved in a northerly direction, Chalons-sur-Marne being one stop. I remember the long avenue of poplar trees that you see so often in France. We parked the vehicles and managed to get into town that night and, of course, some of the men found brothels – quite an eye-opener for young soldiers!

We passed through Le Mans – where the famous racetrack is and eventually

Gondecourt
Headquarters.

arrived in a little village called Gondecourt, about ten miles south of Lille. It had the traditional village square, with a clock in the middle that chimed all night. Our billet that night was in a disused cinema. This again had a concrete floor but this time instead of one in a bed, two of us climbed into our makeshift bed to keep warm. With doubling up, we now had two blankets and two overcoats. The Regiment had various billets in the area.

I remember listening to the radio and heard the news about the battle with the Graf Spee, on the River Plate, in South America. She was a German pocket battleship and had sunk many of our ships carrying vital supplies in the South Atlantic. She had fought three British cruisers – Ajax, Achilles and Exeter, before retreating into Montevideo harbour. The unexpected outcome was when the Graf Spee sailed a short way from shore, before being scuttled by its crew and later her Captain, Hans Langsdorff, committed suicide.

Here we remained from the October (we had landed on the 1st October) until Christmas. On free nights we went into the Estaminet (public house) for coffee and Cognac. We had our Christmas celebrations here and the Naffi sent us some Christmas puddings and other such items that we gratefully received.

I was friendly with Tony Birkbeck, who was the brother of Captain Birkbeck, for whom I was driving. During our free time if we wanted to meet the Captain we had to meet at a private place and usually met in the room behind the bar in the Estaminet. Ordinary ranks were not allowed to mix with officers in those days.

Outside Estaminet, Gondecourt in November 1939.
Back row (l to r) Tony Birkbeck; ? ;
Alec; Lt. Alan Richardson (white coat); ? ;
? ; Donald Wadell: ?

Outside the Estaminet with waitresses and a few locals

We spent our time doing training, drills, parades, and manoeuvres and digging out gun emplacements as well as guard duty. We formed a defence line there in case we had to drop back into action. It was a very wet winter and the gun park where we parked our vehicles was knee-deep in mud!

I got leave in the January (1940) to go back to 'dear old Blighty' (Britain) as it was affectionately known and came home to my parent's house in Lancaster for ten days, where I promptly developed a skin complaint. As a result of this, Doctor Stout, my own doctor, gave me an extra week's extension to my leave. My skin complaint managed to clear up before I was due to go back. Mother, unfortunately, was ill at the time and was in bed with bronchitis. As things turned out I regretted later that I had not seen more of her.

I had looked forward to seeing Norah again and disappointedly found her in bed with measles. She soon recovered and we spent a very happy leave together. I proposed marriage to her but she refused me saying, 'No, I think we are a bit too young. We'll wait!' So that was it and it turned out to be quite a long wait, but well worth it!

We spent the last day of my leave together and we drove up towards Keswick. On the way back, we noticed big black clouds zooming along behind us. Arriving back in Lancaster I quickly got changed and Norah took me to Castle Station where she put me on the night train for London. By this time snow was falling fast and furiously – hence the zooming black clouds. This was to mark the beginning of the severe winter of 1940.

The train was due out at 7 pm but the railway line was blocked with snow just south of Lancaster at Bailrigg so the train just sat in the station for three hours. Norah stayed with me. (I learned later that her parents were not too pleased!) Eventually we set off and the train took sixteen hours before it finally arrived at Euston Station. The RTO (Railway Transport Officer) was the army officer in charge of rail transport. He checked to make sure I had an authentic reason for arriving late and he gave us (other service men) a certificate that covered us. We made our way down to Dover and sailed to Boulogne and then by train to Gondecourt. We found that the Regiment had left and gone on manoeuvres. The troop train that we had travelled on from Boulogne had a lot of its windows broken and this had been caused accidentally by soldiers - their steel helmets were carried on their packs on their backs and when they turned or were squashed this was the outcome!

We caught up with the Regiment and continued with the same routine as before. At the beginning of April we were moved to a new position in Lille.

Soldiers of the British Commonwealth!
Soldiers of the United States of America!

The great Bolshevik offensive has now crossed the frontiers of Germany. The men in the Moscow Kremlin believe the way is open for the conquest of the Western world. This will certainly be the decisive battle for us. But it will also be the decisive battle for England, for the United States and for the maintenance of Western civilisation.

Or whatever today remains of it.

The events in the Baltic States, in Poland, Hungary and Greece are proof enough for us all to see the real program behind the mask of Moscow's socalled **"limited national aims"** and reveals to us how Moscow interprets democratic principles both for the countries she has conquered and also for Germany and **for your countries as well.**

It is also clear enough **today** that the issue at stake is not merely the destruction of Germany and the extermination of the German race. **The fate of your country too is at stake.** This means the fate of your wives, of your children, your home. It also means everything that make life livable, lovable and honorable for you.

Each one of you who has watched the development of Bolshevism throughout this war knows in his innermost heart the truth about Bolshevism. Therefore we are now addressing you as white men to other white men. This is not an appeal. At least we feel there is no alternative for any of us, who feels himself a citizen of our continent and our civilisation but to stop the red flood here and now.

Extraordinary events demand extraordinary measures and decisions. One of these decisions is now put up to you. We address ourselves to you regardless of your rank or of your nationality.

Soldiers! We are sure there are some amongst you who have recognized the danger of Bolshevik-Communism for his own country. We are sure that many of you have seen clearly what this war is now leading to. **We are sure that many of you see what the consequences of the destruction of Europe — not just of Germany but of Europe — will mean to your own country.** Therefore we want to make the following proposal to all of you.

We think that our fight has also become your fight. If there are some amongst you who are willing to take consequences and who are willing to join the ranks of the German soldiers who fight in this battle which will decide both the fate of Germany and the fate of your countries we should like to know it. We invite you to join our ranks and the tens of thousands of volunteers from the communist crushed and conquered nations of eastern Europe, which have had to choose between submission under an most brutal asiatic rule — or a national existence in the future under European ideas, many of which, of course are your own ideals.

Whether you are willing to fight in the front-line or in the service corps: we make you this solemn promise: Whoever as a soldier of his own nation is willing to join the common front for the common cause, will be freed immediately after the victory of the present offensive and can return to his own country via Switzerland.

All that we have to ask from you is the word of the gentleman not to fight directly or indirectly for the cause of Bolshivik-Communism so long as this war continues.

At this moment we do not ask you to think about Germany. We ask you to think about your own country, we ask you just to measure the chances which you and your people at home would have to, in case the Bolshivik - Communism onslaught should overpower Europe. We must and we will put an end to Bolshevism and we will achieve this under all circumstances. Please inform the convoy-officer of your decision and you will receive the priviliges of our own men for we expect you to share their duty. This is something which surpasses all national bounderies. The world today is confronted by the fight of the east against the west. We ask you to think it over.

Are you for the culture of West or the barbaric asiatic East?

Make your decision now!

Propaganda leaflet dropped by the Germans

French money issued (possibly by the Germans) during wartime

We were stationed in a car park and garages with our vehicles and billeted in quite a decent house in Lille. We dug more gun emplacements, going out on exercises, numerous car duties and drills as usual.

Here the French people were very nice and friendly to us, inviting us in for coffee when we had a break. We became friendly with the Wacheux family. The father was the local wine merchant who supplied the officers' mess with their booze. He had a contract for bringing over bottled Bass Beer and Red Bass that was a particularly lovely quality. He was married, with a wife, daughter Paulette and son Jackie. I became very friendly with the whole family. Paulette would only be about twelve and Jackie a little older.

One of our lighter moments I remember, whilst we were there, was one evening we went to the fairground at Tourcoing. We were due back at our billets in Lille at 10 pm and would be checked. There was a tram that ran between the two towns. We had a few drinks and were feeling rather foolhardy. We jumped onto the tram and rushed up to the front where the driver was standing and grabbing hold of the tram handle brought it forward at great speed. It seemed to fuse the tram and it immediately stopped. We all jumped off and ran the rest of the way back to our barracks.

The Germans dropped propaganda leaflets from planes but the Allied Soldiers just ignored them. I still have a copy of one I picked up.

On the 12th May, we hadn't been there very long when Jerry (Germans) broke through the Low Countries (Belgium and Holland) and we were called into action. We travelled during the night in convoy to the Belgium frontier. A few times we were bombed and strafed (machine-gun fired at close range from a low flying aircraft) quite considerably but fortunately we didn't have any casualties, but numerous times we had to disembark and dive into the ditches for cover!

8 cwt 4-wheeled personnel or wireless truck (Humber) just like the one Alec drove.

A 25-pounder gun-howitzer, showing the method of towing and limber.

We had one very big battle with the Germans at Louvain, near Brussels, lasting three days. Jerry had broken through in great force with enormous tanks that nearly surrounded us. We managed to drop into action and were firing a salvo (simultaneous discharge of two or more guns) and we were very nearly captured.

We were told to withdraw, so we withdrew gradually back through France, dropping into action at various places, in orchards, farms etc. We had a severe aerial attack and strafing where we lost many vehicles and equipment. We managed to withdraw safely eventually arriving back in Lille to us this was a great disappointment. We went into action again in our own gun emplacements, which we had already prepared. This proved to be a very heavy battle.

Eventually we had to retreat to the coast to Dunkirk from where we expected to be evacuated but no, it was not to be. The Regiment consisted of six troops and our headquarters. Our troop, (E' Troop), F' Troop and another troop were ordered to do a rearguard action to defend Dunkirk and the remainder were told to be prepared to evacuate to Britain.

We were given positions to go to and I was driving our vehicle with our officer-in-charge, Captain Maurice Birkbeck in the front passenger seat. There was a large fire and houses were well alight. We skirted round them only to be confronted by large German Panzer tanks with the same sized guns (25-pounders) that we had behind. It would have taken us some time to take them off the vehicle and bring them into action. At this point we were unfortunately captured. We were ordered out of our vehicles and were now in the arms of the Germans.

The Don R (dispatch rider – who was directing us) was running along beside our vehicles on his motorbike quickly summed up the situation and managed to quickly turn his bike around and make off back without the Germans even seeing him. Likewise two other guns and the maintenance vehicle behind us were able to go into a cornfield and turn round and retreat.

The officer in the rear vehicle was called Richardson, he had managed to withdraw even though he had been given orders by his Captain to go into action and didn't. Nevertheless, had he done so we would probably all have been killed. In not doing so he had disobeyed orders, retreated back and was evacuated from Dunkirk. He was court-martialled and discharged from the army back into 'Civvy Street' to work in the factories – which was a terrible thing really! The Don R, Sergeant Gardiner, was so upset by the whole thing that he committed suicide.

Chapter Six

Prisoner of War – Stalag VIII B

The 28th May, 1940 marked the beginning of my captivity. Having been ordered out of our vehicles we stood there in our battledress and were ordered to march to a meeting centre. This turned out to be a village church and there we met up with many other troops, including F' Troop and hundreds of other soldiers. We were marched off in a long procession, German soldiers riding along on their motorbikes and sidecars, with mounted machine guns and many other military vehicles. We had been captured at six o'clock that morning and we marched all day without being given anything to eat. At nine o'clock that night, they opened a field gate and just ushered us in. We just lay down exhausted and totally wet through.

There were a few French cauldrons (large metal pots) of soup available next morning but with hundreds of us to feed very few of us got any. The following day we marched continuously away from the front and the coastline in the direction of Germany. We marched along the line of the roads – not on the actual roads, as these were full of heavy convoys of dust-laden vehicles and supplies heading for the front. Sometimes we did manage to dive into a ditch and get a drink of water to quench our thirst. When we marched through the villages, the civilians were ushered away if they tried to offer us food or help.

One of our billets was St. Omer Prison. I was on the first floor and a shot was fired off down below and the bullet came up through the floorboard beside me. Obviously a German had shot over the head of a prisoner. I remember passing the Somme Cemetery where 60,000 comrades lay, lost during the First World War. Escape was out of the question as there were too many guards.

We finally arrived in Trier to see all the Swastika flags and bunting out – marking the day that France had fallen – capitulated. There was jubilation among the people but all we got was 'Boos!' We were sent up the hill to the ex-army barracks only to find hundreds and hundreds of French and British soldiers assembled and waiting. Over the next three or four days, a certain amount of food was given to us, this consisted mainly of soup. We had had very little food on the march apart from what we could scrounge in certain places where we stayed. We had been able to obtain a bit of bread and boiled eggs from civilians and even resorted to eating any turnips we could find in the fields.

Eventually we were taken from the prison at Trier down to the railway sidings and ordered to climb into box trucks. These had been used in the First World War and were meant to hold forty men or six horses but they piled sixty of us in. Consequently we were squashed and couldn't all sit down, some had to stand up. By this time, we all had dysentery from drinking water in the drainage ditches – it was frightful as you can imagine. There was one slit (opening) in the truck that we used as a latrine, which was helpful! We were halted at certain stations – Leipzig was one. The door was opened and some black/green mouldy bread was thrown in to us. Whilst we were here, Sturton (family were solicitors in Lancaster), one of the soldiers from our Regiment, tried to escape running across the railway line but was shot.

It took us three days to cross Germany before we arrived at Stalag VIII B – the Prisoner of War (PoW) Camp, in Silesia, between Poland and Germany. This was a large industrial area that the Germans had taken over and were utilising all the coal, making oil and many other by-products from it. Stalag VIII B was heavily guarded, surrounded by a large barbed wire fence with lookout posts armed with machine guns and was always lit up at night.

This was the main camp for all the British prisoners in that area. Australians and New Zealanders joined us but they were later drafted to other camps. There were Polish prisoners in an adjoining camp. It was also to this camp that prisoners were sent back for whatever reason and from there they would be redistributed to another working party or they were investigated and dealt with accordingly. This was a very large camp in which there must have been thousands of prisoners.

We were issued a pre-printed letter post card written in German with Stalag VIIIB and stated, 'I am well. I am a German war prisoner. I feel very well. Very best wishes.' I printed my name, PoW number and addressed the card to my mother and father and I was able to send it home on the 20th June, 1940 (I was captured 28th May, 1940). My father and mother received it on the 5th September, 1940. Father translated the German and wrote in English above it. During all these months they didn't know whether I was alive or dead!

Father told me later that he had been at Penrith Auction Mart that day and had told the auctioneer, Jack Proctor, whom he knew very well, that after all the months of worry and uncertainty, 'Great news! I heard this morning that my son is safe and he is a prisoner.' There was great joy when they announced it in the selling ring and he celebrated that day with a lot of other farmers at Penrith Agricultural Hall.

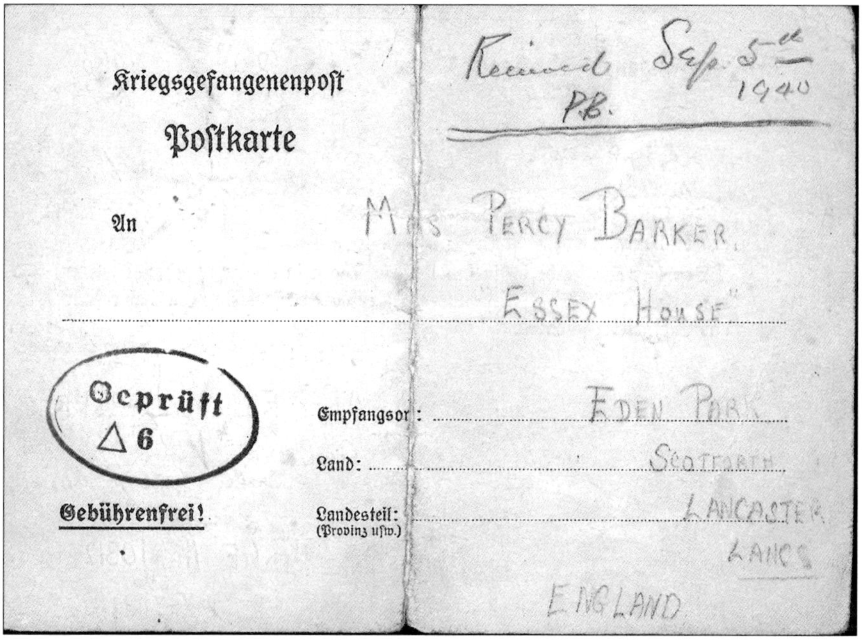

Kriegsgefangenenpost

Postkarte

Received Sep. 5th 1940 P.B.

An

Mrs Percy Barker.

"Essex House"

Geprüft △ 6

Gebührenfrei!

Empfangsort: Eden Park

Land: Scotforth

Landesteil: (Provinz usw.) Lancaster

Lancs

England

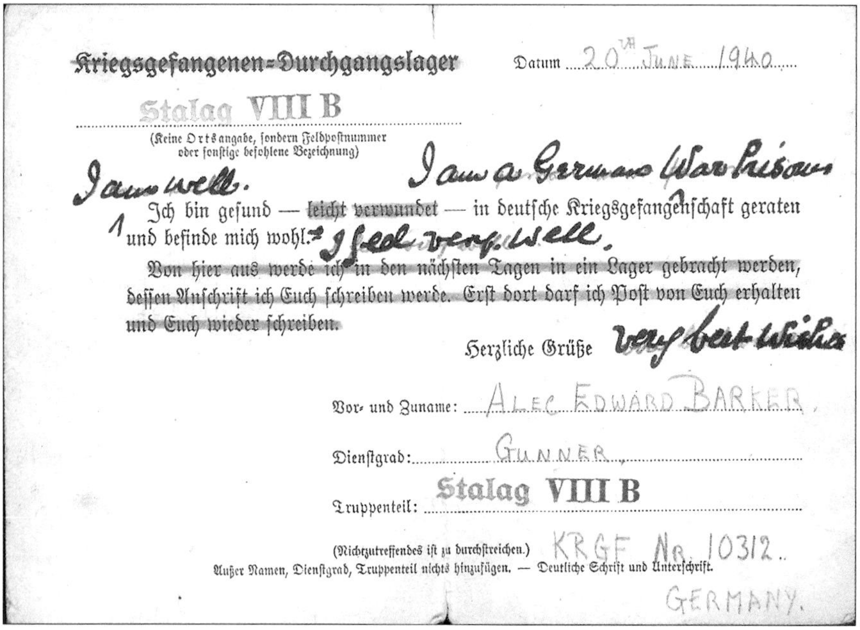

Kriegsgefangenen-Durchgangslager

Datum 20th June 1940

Stalag VIII B

(Keine Ortsangabe, sondern Feldpostnummer oder sonstige befohlene Bezeichnung)

I am well. *I am a German War Prisoner*

Ich bin gesund — leicht verwundet — in deutsche Kriegsgefangenschaft geraten und befinde mich wohl. *I feel very well.*

Von hier aus werde ich in den nächsten Tagen in ein Lager gebracht werden, dessen Anschrift ich Euch schreiben werde. Erst dort darf ich Post von Euch erhalten und Euch wieder schreiben.

Herzliche Grüße *very best wishes*

Vor- und Zuname: Alec Edward Barker.

Dienstgrad: Gunner

Stalag VIII B

Truppenteil:

(Nichtzutreffendes ist zu durchstreichen.) KRGF Nr. 10312.

Außer Namen, Dienstgrad, Truppenteil nichts hinzufügen. — Deutsche Schrift und Unterschrift.

GERMANY.

Copy of the card Alec sent home on 20th June 1940 to say he was alive and a prisoner.

28

Group picture taken of prisoners from Alec's hut so it could be sent home to show how well they all looked. Back row 2nd from left Jim McCabe. 2nd back row Gilbert and Alec. Front row 2nd from right ? McMann.

IPSWICH MEN PRISONERS

PREVIOUSLY REPORTED MISSING

Mr. and Mrs. Jay of 12, Kingston Road, Ipswich, have been notified that their son, Pte W. Jay of the Green Howards, reported wounded May 29th and later reported missing on June 20th, is now a prisoner of war in Germany.

Driver L. L. Luck, R.E., second son of Mr. and Mrs. Luck, 62, Pauline Street, Ipswich, previously reported missing, presumed killed, is now officially reported a prisoner in Germany.

Mr. and Mrs. Percy Barker, of Eden Park, Lancaster, who formerly lived at Stoke Park, Ipswich, have received a communication that their son, Gunner Alec Edward Barker, is a prisoner of war. He was previously reported as missing at Dunkirk on May 28th. The communication is dated, June 20th, 1940, and addressed from Stalag VIII. B.

Their eldest son, Mr. Owen Percy Barker, has been gazetted 2nd-Lieut. in the Royal Regiment of Artillery. He is in civil life a member of the London Stock Exchange, and joined the Forces in April, 1939.

German stamp on back of above photograph - they stamped all photographs with PoW camp details.

Article that went in the local Ipswich newspaper re the news of Alec being a PoW and mention of Owen.

With days with no, or very little, food we were now very hungry and we could literally count our ribs! Also as a result of the terrible conditions we had suffered and lack of any sanitary facilities we were lousy. They shaved our heads and we were photographed. These photographs were taken showing our prison camp numbers on our chests – mine was No. 10312. They punched our number on a small piece of soft oblong metal and this was attached to a length of string round our necks. Our clothing was put into a steamer with the sole purpose that it would kill these dreadful lice. Unfortunately this was not the case

Owen Barker in officer's uniform.

as the eggs the lice had laid were still on our bodies and they just hatched out again, so we were never really free of them. At certain times they had fleas to keep them company, which burrowed into the blankets at night and came out to chase you round in bed! They were indeed very unpleasant.

Our rations at Stalag VIII B were just enough to exist on - so many grams of bread, a small knob of margarine and a bowl of soup. The soup could be anything from just water and potatoes, to a bit of pork rind floating in it! This was not good food but they were adhering to the Geneva Convention – they were feeding us!

Later we were informed that all non-commissioned officers should work – as laid down again by the Geneva Convention. Men were formed into working parties and were later sent out to work and live in the different labour camps made up of usually two hundred and fifty soldiers. They asked me what I did in 'Civvy Street' and of course I said something appertaining to farming, and with that they sent me to a labour camp (later to a coal mine) with five hundred others. Whereas the French whom I think were all industrial people went on the farms – but no that was the German way of treating people fairly or unfairly as the case maybe!

Chapter Seven

Labour Camp – down the Coal Mine

My first working party from the labour camp was involved in digging and building the foundations of a factory for Siemens, the large German electrical firm. This was really hard labour and we had half an hour's march to the site, then twelve hours work – labouring all the time before the half hour march back at night. By then our boots were worn out and they supplied us with some Dutch clogs they had managed to obtain from somewhere in Holland. We had no socks and we improvised and used what we called 'foot lappings' – that were simply square pieces of rag wrapped round each foot. We still had no Red Cross parcels and every day we were keenly awaiting their arrival. A large barbed wire fence surrounded the camp with guards and Alsatian dogs patrolling all the time around the outside perimeter. Our outside latrine was just a covered shed, which had a large pit down below with a plank across the top. Any newspapers available were adapted for that use!

What we were required to do was just sheer hard manual labour, digging soil and stone out with a long handled spade and levelling the ground. We had a little tipping truck that we filled with soil, pushed it along the small narrow gauge lines to where there was a hole which required filling with soil and tipped it up and into it. The small length of line was periodically moved and assembled to the next piece of ground that required work doing to it. The only other mechanical device was a steam loader (like a JCB) used for digging holes etc.

Our next move was in November 1940 to Work Camp E22. This was some distance from the main camp. We were to work at the Herman Goering Werks coal mine at Oehringen between Gleiwitz and Hindenburg. There were about two hundred and fifty prisoners in the camp, five huts each with fifty or so men. We were wakened at 5 o'clock every morning by the guard knocking on the door and then opening it and shouting in German, 'Raus! Raus!'(Get out! Get out!). We would get up, splash our faces with water from the tap and get into our uniforms ready for the day ahead.

At 6 am we were called outside to 'Aufstellung'! (Line-up) and we had roll call and we were counted. This done we would be brought to attention and marched out of the camp in correct order. We were only about quarter-of-a-mile from the coal mine and on reaching it, we would march across to the camp and through the gatehouse where our numbers were clocked in and, of course, we would go through the same procedure at night. We then went

Hermen Goering Werks coal mine with the weighbridge on the right.

Group of PoWs standing in front of a pithead wagon.
Back row (l to r)   ?   Alec;   Gilbert;   ?   British PoW
Front row   ?   British Pow and   ?   a Russians PoW.

into the changing rooms and took off our uniforms, let down a long chain from the ceiling that had hooks on it, where our overalls etc were hanging from the previous day.

Initially, when they sent us to the mine my first job was working on the surface moving rails. We used to have to move the sections of rails and the sleepers at the sidings near the pithead and laid new lines for the trains. We carried the rails and sleepers on our shoulders. This equated to one man per foot of rail or sleeper and the tallest bore the brunt of the weight (of which I was one) – it was pretty hard going I can tell you!

One day when I was running across the line I tripped and sprained my ankle and I was unable to walk. This turned out to be quite fortunate as the doctor said that I was unfit for work and was confined to barracks.

Whilst there I was resting and besides getting my daily ration, I used to go out to the adjoining camp where the guards lived and one of the guards seemed to take pity on me and gave me a bowl of soup every day. This helped to improve matters a little bit. Then I was back to work.

My next job was working down the mine. In the morning, after we had changed we went to the pithead ready to be drafted into small gangs. The way they worked was quite simple, a German would pick you out and this equated to one German, one prisoner and one Polish labourer. The three of us worked and, of course, the German

One of the friendly German soldiers

was on piecework. So naturally the harder he made us work, the more money he made. It was a disastrous set up from our point of view. I was working in a very deep shaft that had a 45° slope, with a metre high seam. We used carbide lamps, as there were no explosive gases. We were taken in a coal truck to the coalface and we had to shovel coal down to the hopper – gruelling work. At times I disappeared into the dark but was soon found by the German and he knocked me about. Next day, the same ganger for obvious reasons did not choose me!

PoW Working Parties.

At night when we came out of the mine we did at least have a hot shower and changed out of the overalls back into our uniforms and marched back to camp. The same guard marched back with us and he would have been on duty with us all day wherever we were.

Alec at the coal mine by a pithead wagon.

Every labour camp had a cookhouse whereby we were summoned by bell from the huts to go out and collect our meals. We took with us our own bowls to get our soup and we were issued with 400 grams of black bread, 25 grams white cheese, ½ a sausage and a knob of margarine. During our meal we would sit down and have a chat and if by then we had our Red Cross parcels, we would substitute our meagre rations for something we would be able to cook for ourselves on a flat stove, which was in the corner of each hut. This was something we would do in turns.

Each camp had a sergeant who acted as their spokesman. He was accompanied by an interpreter, an Englishman who could speak German. I had learnt German initially at school and obviously was picking up more German as time went along, as it was to my and others' advantage and I can still speak it today! I also learnt quite a few words in Polish but found it more difficult to learn and it really wasn't necessary. The people we were working with were Polish, but had a very good knowledge of German – so German was the main language used. None of these people I was with and did little deals with spoke English – so it was definitely to our advantage to learn to speak German as soon as we could. I picked up languages pretty quickly but George Hemsworth was better. (He stayed on afterwards in the Army as he was a regular, and was an interpreter in the Occupation Army, in Germany). I spoke a little bit of French when I was in France but there was none spoken in camp.

Inside our huts we had double bunks and lay on straw palliasse (mattress) and had one blanket each. It was a very severe winter. Fortunately, we had a large round stove in the middle with a pipe at the top that went out through the roof and that kept us warm. There was no shortage of coal so that was one good thing. As well as the flat open stove in the corner, we had a water tap for drinking or washing and a large bucket in another corner as a latrine. Two of us shared a cupboard for storage.

I obtained a large wooden chest (not sure how!) for three mates and myself who shared everything from cigarettes to Red Cross parcels for the duration - George Hemsworth, Jim McCabe from Perth and Gilbert (Jock from Aberdeen). We all had our uses, I did a little bit of bartering and Jim was the barber and was the chatterbox. George was the organiser and came up with some good ideas. Our other Scots friend, Jock was the cook and did most of the cooking for us.

Another day when I was returning from work at the coal mine, I was searched as usual at the gate by one of the guards. Unfortunately he found a kilo loaf of bread that I was trying to smuggle in and back to our hut. It was rather a long loaf, as French bread used to be, and the Germans had made it, so it was black. I had obtained it from one of my friendly Polish civilians, cut it in half and put one half down each side of my trousers. When searching they don't normally go down as far as that but on this occasion the guard found the bread. I was, of course, taken to the commandant and he interviewed me and said, 'From whom did you get that bread?' He was very interested in a certain civilian, because it was a very serious offence if anyone was caught giving any food to the prisoners. Food was a very valuable commodity in Germany as it was very scarce. I said, 'I found it on the railway line where I was working!' He didn't believe me, of course, and continued to interrogate me but I stuck to my story. He said, 'Right, if you don't tell me the name of the man you will go into solitary confinement until you do.' So that's where I went. It was a dark room with one small window at the top and a bunk bed to lie on. There was a bin in the corner for nature's necessities and the guard would come in once a day and give me my slightly reduced rations.

The first day I slept, it was a lovely rest but after that it became very tedious and boredom set in. Day became night and night became day. I was taken out and interrogated and asked the same question again but I still gave the same answer. 'I found the bread on the railway line.' I knew he didn't believe me but he couldn't disprove it. Eventually, after four days, which were pretty awful really, they released me and I went back to normal duties.

I worked in the coal mine down below the surface for about six weeks and then we had a medical examination by a German arzt (doctor). Again this was part of the Geneva Convention to see if we were fit to work or not. During my childhood I had a perforated eardrum after having quinsy and tonsillitis and the doctor perforated my ear. I pointed this out to the doctor 'I can't hear properly and I am in pain' and continued by saying, 'I don't like being down in the claustrophobic conditions with this ear trouble.' After my visit I got permission to work on the surface and I never went down a coal mine again, thank God!

The prisoners who worked on the surface did day shift and they all had similar health problems which allowed them to do this. The others did three shifts a day like some of my friends who shared the same hut. George Hemsworth also worked on the surface. George, as mentioned, had joined the army as a regular and was an artificer - he looked after the mechanics of the guns.

In November 1940 we had problems because all the slag that was coming out of the coal mines was freezing in the trucks, as the weather was so severe. We were getting down to 20° plus of frost. Our job was to empty the frozen trucks. They provided us with gloves, for if we touched the metal with our bare skin it would just come off. We also wore any other clothing we had, such as balaclavas and scarves.

Another job was loading some of the twenty-ton wagons with coal dust from the hoppers. I used to purposely overload these as often as possible, so that the coal trains would be delayed as the weight had to be adjusted – all taking more time! The poor horses that used to come to the coal mines had icicles hanging down from their nostrils. So you can just imagine how very, very cold it was!

After a while I was drafted to the Holtz Platz wood yard. Here we had a little hut where we donned our clothes and everything, usually in the dark. This yard was where they kept the wooden props for the mine. They were stacked and stored ready for use down the pit to prop up the roof. These were unloaded from wagons which arrived from Villach (forestry region of Austria) with the various sized pit props. These were stacked inside the wagon and had to be lifted out through the middle door, placed into buggies and wheeled along a little track and put into stacks according to size and length until they were required down the mine. Later in the day the order would come through from the foreman specifying the size and quantity of pit props he required. These were loaded into buggies and pushed down to the pithead and left there for them.

There was a large prop measuring eighteen inches (46 cm) by five foot long (153 cm) – it was some animal! Sometimes there would be two of us but other times you had to struggle on your own. They all varied in size from the small to very large.

George Hemsworth in the wood yard.

Military funeral given to three young soldiers who tried to escape.

Whenever we left or returned to camp we tried to confuse the guard whilst he was counting. Another ruse was faking ill health whenever possible so that we were unable to work for obvious reasons. One trick was simply putting broken up aspirin into a cigarette and when smoked this would cause you to have heart palpitations.

I was once asked 'Why didn't we escape?' Well we were taught a very sad lesson in that very first week when we arrived at the coal mine. Three of my friends decided they would walk out of the camp, it was as simple as that. Indeed it was very tempting for everybody. It was quite easy then as they had not got it properly guarded and the three of them just disappeared into the wood. They were shot dead for trying to escape. Their bodies were brought back to camp to serve, as an example of what happened to would be escapees. In the middle of Europe there wasn't a lot of opportunity for us and I didn't know anything about maps or anything like that. The lads were given a full military funeral – it was terrible – you just never forget things like that.

Non-commissioned officers in Stalag VIII B – working party E22 (Alec's). Standing in doorway, at back, is Sergeant Major who was the spokesman and in charge.

Russian PoWs who also worked in the coal mine

Chapter Eight

The Red Cross

The Red Cross were wonderful to us during my five years in camp and I, like all the other prisoners, owe them a great debt of gratitude. There were many aspects to their work and they undoubtedly helped us through those awful years. Whereby they importantly helped to keep our spirits up and even enabled us to do a spot of bartering at which I proved to be quite good! I think my father can take some of the credit for that!

It was six months before we received our first Red Cross parcels. By that time we had gone almost to skeletons – I was now six and a half stone and we could count every rib in our body. We had been working very hard and living on very scanty rations. On top of all that was the tremendous stress in simply not knowing what was happening and what the future held for us.

The main thing, of course, was the food parcel. What they tried to achieve was to get through to each of us a ten-pound (approx. 5 kilos) parcel of food every week but, of course, this didn't happen for various reasons. After they arrived they were dished out to us from a hut and, if there were not one for each of us, we would share a parcel between groups of us. It was very irregular and sometimes you didn't get anything for a month or two, some must simply have gone astray.

These parcels contained most of the things that were not available in Germany e.g. tea, coffee, butter, sugar, chocolate, dried milk (Klim), meat loaf, fish tins, soap, Virginia cigarettes and all those ingredients that would help to make things bearable. So with the meagre rations we got, the Red Cross really did help to save our lives. They were also responsible for getting through to us new uniforms etc which we were allowed from the army. We could now start to become human beings again and think and dream about girls, not just food and bars of chocolate!

The other important thing of course was correspondence – letters and parcels. They were responsible for getting this through to us, as well as getting our letters to our loved ones back home. Every three months our families were allowed a special permit from the Red Cross that enabled them to send a personal parcel.

As letters were all censored. Nothing detrimental could be written about the camp or the Germans. We couldn't write any news. We were issued with a letter card once a month. Sometimes letters came through easily, other times not – the transport could have been bombed, there was nothing regular. 'Mail up' they would say and you would go and wait. We used to get news from new prisoners and quiz them for all the latest news – it was good for morale!

Mother sent me warm clothing, a balaclava and gloves she had knitted. Sometimes items would be surplus to requirements and acted as a means of dealing/bartering to enable us to get food for which we were so desperate. One item I received from home was a pair of silk pyjamas, of all things, from father! I don't know what he was thinking about at the time, but it did give us a laugh! Nevertheless, I managed to exchange them for something more useful later on. I was even able to send correspondence to my Aunt Bessie in America. In return she sent me parcels of clothing – she had obtained my PoW number and details from my father.

The Wacheux family who had befriended me in Lille, found out from the Red Cross where I was and sent me food parcels out of their very scanty provisions. Food was a precious commodity everywhere.

Besides clothing in one of my father's parcels he included a round tin of Castella cigars. Every parcel was opened in front of the old commandant and his eyes suddenly lit up! He smoked cigars continuously. He dropped a bit of a hint so I gave him a few. Miraculously, a short time later a new pair of boots were issued to me! He was a very human type of commandant. They were changed regularly, some, as you can imagine, were absolute bastards and we were kept very much under their strict control – others were more lenient and human. The Germans were just like any other race.

Alec, Jim McCabe and Gilbert standing outside their hut.

I was also working with the Polish civilians who were really being used as a form of slave labour by the Germans. They had smallholdings back in Poland and used to go home at weekends. If we gave them maybe a bar of soap, chocolate, cigarettes or coffee which they had never seen, or even a packet of tea that we could probably spare at that particular time, they would bring us back some bulk food, such as bread, potatoes, flour, yeast etc which were items we required. So these carbohydrate foods helped supplement our meagre rations and helped to build us up.

One of our best items for bartering was our own British Virginian cigarettes of which we had a wonderful supply in our Red Cross parcels or separately through our own personal parcels from our parents e.g. Players, Capstan, or large tinned Woodbine – a very nice cigarette known as Naval Woodbine which came in sealed tins of fifty. Everybody smoked and people would give away food for extra cigarettes. We would share a cigarette and the tab end would be saved, broken up and put in a tin. All the tab ends would then be put together and with a cigarette paper we would manage to roll another cigarette from it!

There was an issue of German cigarettes – Polish, actually, consisting of a long cardboard tube with a little bit of tobacco in the end, this was Balkan tobacco, it was horrible stinking stuff!

I could speak German and learned to understand and speak a little Polish. It certainly helped in our daily life and also when I had a little problem with my teeth. My front teeth had been capped when I was at school after a boy had accidentally bumped his head against mine in the swimming pool. I lost some of the gold from one of my teeth and needed a replacement so the local village dentist could repair it. Fortunately, I had met a Polish girl at the weighbridge, near the entrance to the coal mine. I used to talk to her and she was aware that I had lost this gold cap off my tooth. The arrangement was that she was to give me one of her earrings for this. The only problem was passing it to me without the guard seeing it. So we quickly arranged how we were going to do it. At 6 am when we were marching from one camp to another in the dark she surreptitiously came in amongst us and slipped me the earring. Later when the guard took us to the civilian dentist in the village he waited for us in the waiting room. I gave the earring to the dentist who kindly remodelled it and fitted it on my tooth without asking any awkward questions. I gave the girl some coffee in exchange.

E22 Football Team.

E22 Band.

Chapter Nine

Camp Life – the 'Crystal Set'

The people in my hut were from many different regiments and indeed 'all walks of life' and some of them were of a very rough nature. There were two Cockneys who arrived from London and they were known as the 'Racing Gang'. They used to attend the race meetings with the sole purpose of robbing and picking people's pockets – which of course had to lapse for the duration. In fact here in camp they achieved notoriety for quite another pastime and were known as the 'Razor Gang' and this was how it came about. One of these lads went to work one day while his mate was on another shift. He cunningly went off with his mate's boots to sell to a civilian. When he got back his mate was naturally not too happy and attacked him with a cut-throat razor. He went for his throat and the lad put his hand up to shield himself and the razor caught him on his lower arm. That of course was the end of the pair of them. They were sent back to the main camp Stalag VIII B and we never saw them again. Where he got the razor from I don't know, all I do know is that you could obtain certain things from strange places and no questions were asked – you were just pleased that the item was there and could be put to the purpose for which it was required.

Our camps were made up of British soldiers, English, Scottish, Welsh, and Irish and there were some real characters amongst them. The Welsh Guards I remember very well. One fellow was known as 'The Schneider' – German for tailor, he used to sew on our buttons and do any other needlework we required and payment would be a cigarette!

Some of the men became mentally ill. This could have been caused through what they had seen or been put through, or the conditions we were in not knowing what would happen or when the war would eventually end and who would win, though naturally we hoped it would be us! A lot depended on your own make-up and stamina. I can remember one poor fellow picking the lice from himself and eating them – we were all lousy but that was something else! He was also sent back to main camp. We had all kinds.

Another thing that the Geneva Convention stipulated was that prisoners had to be paid in camp money, so much a month. This was paper money that could only be spent in the local shop and one or two occupants of the hut would be elected to run that canteen. I was one of three who ran the canteen in our hut with my two friends George Hemsworth and Jim McCabe. We had a little four-wheeled buggy with a shaft at the front that

Jim McCabe cutting George Hemsworth's hair.

E22 Hot Shots band in action.

enabled one of us to pull and the other two pushed whilst the guard marched beside us. Occasionally if one of us was busy another member from the hut would come instead. We would take the orders and money from the rest in our hut and go with the guard down to the village shop, owned by an old lady called Frau Chunka. Then we would bring back what they required. Of course we were limited to what was available

The four-wheeled buggy used to go to the village shop. Alec behind with ? and Jim McCabe on right.

Everything was rationed and there was never any food available. Usually we got cigarette papers, pencils, note books and could get mirrors and razors for shaving with. We purchased our goods and maybe we bought some other items that could be sold later on to the boys. The perk from Frau Chunka was the little bottle of Schnapps that she would often put in the bottom of the box for us - which we greatly enjoyed when we got back to camp.

We even managed to make some Schnapps – it's great what one can think up! We sometimes got currants in the Red Cross parcels and were able to obtain potatoes from the civilians and together with some enterprising boys in the camp we were able to ferment this. I got some yeast from one of my Polish friends. We put potatoes, currants and sugar and anything else we could think of into a large container to start the fermentation process. One of the lads made a still out of some Red Cross tins. He got an old kettle from somewhere and soldered the spout, numerous things happened – small miracles really! We fermented this stuff and put it in a still and ran it through the piping and cooled it down with cold water, then raw alcohol came out at the other end! So we had a still of our own in our little hut. This was neat alcohol and we let it down with something else, either some coffee or water or other ingredients we had managed to get hold of. This went on for quite a number of months until one of the guards unfortunately came in and found it. It was confiscated but we firmly believed they used it for themselves after that!

Inside the hut during Christmas

Christmas Pantomime.

Christmas time was pantomime season. Men would dress up in drag. We were able to purchase accordions with our camp money. The music was wonderful and the costumes were made from blankets and any old clothes from home. We really had some very clever and imaginative chaps! The pantomimes they put on were superb and kept people's peckers up and gave them something else to think about!

One day I received some very sad news from home that my mother had died in March 1943. I learned she had a very serious illness, and Norah had taken her to Christies in Manchester for treatment. Dr Stewart who lived next door to our house had been brilliant.

In camp we were fortunate to have a watchmaker and he had knowledge of making small items and we contrived the idea of making a 'crystal set' as we had heard that it was possible to pick up radio signals from London – if we could only get a set made?

When I was working at the wood yard (pit props) I was often in contact with the Polish civilians doing small deals, usually with my little agent and friend, a

Mazur on his wedding day.

little man called Mazur whose home was 15 kilometres away. He used to go home at the weekends and he was able to do bits of business for me, as mentioned before by exchanging soap or cigarettes etc for something we required – he could get me most things. Importantly he was able to obtain a crystal for me and a stolen headphone from the military – with the stipulation that it must be strong in order to receive a good reception.

So the clever watchmaker put these two things together and made me a crystal set with which I was able to receive a signal from London. Broadcasts were made quarter hourly in four different languages, Polish, French, German and English. The station I listened to was called 'Voice of America'. The set was made from an old shaving stick holder and wrapped with copper wire tightly around its 4-inch (10 cm) length. We then neatly fitted it into a small wooden box approximately 7 inches (18 cm) by 4 inches (10 cm). The box, importantly, held the crystal and cat's whisker - the little piece of wire that moved around the crystal. We created a very long aerial by using some disused telephone wires and of course we had our powerful headphone with 1½ inches (4 cm) metal earpiece – courtesy of the German Army! You could hear just like a normal wireless set – you moved the crystal – there was a pin (cat's whisker) on the crystal and a coil altered the frequency. This was a very fluctuating bad signal, consequently it used to go in and out and it took quite a long time to compile a bulletin noting the movement of our troops etc and any other interesting points of news – some of which was pretty terrible. We never actually believed the thousands of tons of shipping (convoys) that were supposedly being sunk weekly in the Atlantic. I read this valuable news out to the rest of the camp.

I still have three news bulletins that I wrote down as I was picking it up from the crystal set. One was dated the BBC News 24th March, 1945 – this, of course, was after we left the camp – the reception was becoming better.

Special News – Montgomery Headquarters announced today that strong Allied Forces crossed the Rhine at 11 am on a very wide front on the north of the Rhine by Wessel. A strong bridgehead had been formed. This second invasion of Germany was preceded by a mass bombing and the greatest artillery barrage of the War's history. 1500 Allied transport planes landed at the airbase – troops who were immediately supplied by Allied Liberators and gliders. Already Allied planes have put 15 German airports in this section out of action rending the German Airforce useless!

If I had been caught this would have been disastrous, likewise the consequences. One of the very strict orders we were given was that no one was allowed to listen to anything coming from Europe and especially Britain. I suppose it was all to do with morale and they didn't want us to know what was happening. The crystal set certainly helped us.

We were always intent on keeping the two main ingredients – the headphone and the crystal hidden. We cut the headphone cable in half. We took the heel of my boot and made a false compartment, hid half the cable in one heel and the crystal we put in the other one with the other half of the cable. That ensured that if anything was found they wouldn't realise or find out really what we had. The aerial we hid in the hut and it was moved around to various locations.

I managed to carry the set with me the whole of the time that I was a prisoner and I still have the set to this day. It has recently been repaired, thanks to a friend, Don Hey, who was with the IBM computer firm for many years and has enabled me to still receive a signal after all these years!

Chapter Ten

The March and Freedom at Last!

Things continued much the same, week by week, in the camp. We had an idea that the Russians were making a big advance on the Eastern Front and we heard the guns in the distance all afternoon. We thought there was something amiss but weren't able to understand what was happening or where they were. Rumour got round that we were to be moved but nothing else was known.

Our suspicions proved to be correct and later guards told us that we were going on a march. We were given instructions that we would be leaving the work camp. We were told that we would be marching to an unknown destination and that we had to take what we could carry on our backs.

At 10 pm on the 22nd January, 1945 the guards forced us out of the huts, lined us up and marched us off into the dark. There were two hundred and fifty of us from our camp. Stalag VIIIB was the main camp and we were all split up over the area in different work camps. When we marched other PoWs joined us. We all walked, there were no lorries and the guards from our camp marched with us to begin with, although they were later changed. The original ones, the severe guards had been drafted to the Eastern Front and the older ones (or crocks) some of whom had been to the Eastern Front and suffered frostbite and other disabilities were now put in charge of us. They were much more lenient with us.

There was severe frost and the road surface was covered with snow and ice. We marched for twenty hours and managed to stop sometimes in a village. I was able to slip into a house at times to warm up and maybe get a cup of coffee. The first night we managed a little sleep in a hut but I remember wakening up with my boots frozen to my feet and thinking, 'Oh, I've got frost bite!' Fortunately no, I was okay and we set off again.

Another twenty-four hours passed before we were eventually put into a farmyard and we had to find our own places to sleep. On other occasions, if we could, we went into barns and on one occasion we were even sleeping with the cows in a cowshed, deriving some heat from them! Small rations of bread and soup were provided but not much, so we tried whenever possible to supplement this to keep up our strength. Usually we could obtain some extra food from the nearest hen hut. My knowledge of farming helped and enabled me to run in and catch a hen or two and quickly wring their necks. It wasn't long before we had the feathers off and into a pan of

Alec showing me how his crystal set worked.

BBC News   March 24th 1945

8 am Special News Montgomery's H.Q. annosed today.
That Strong Allied forces crossed the Rhine at 1-1
on a wide front North of the Rhine by Wessel.
A Strong bridge lead has been formed. This 2nd
Invasion of Germany was preceded by a mass bombing
and the greatest artillery barrage of the Wars history.
1500 Allied transport planes landed the air borne
troops who were imediatly supplied by Allied
Liberators & gliders. Already Allied planes have
put 15 German air fields in this sector out of
action rendering the enemy Air defence useless

Copy of Alec's bulletin which he wrote 60 years ago.

boiling water. Somebody else would maybe find some potatoes about the farm and we had a meal that way. I remember on one occasion going into a hen hut and the guard must have spotted me and came in and ousted me out with the butt of his rifle. Fortunately, that was the only penalty I got!

The four of us, George, Jim, Jock and myself had brought our wooden chest with us, it was approximately four foot (122 cm) long by three foot (91 cm) high and two foot (61 cm) wide. We had it packed with our treasures. In my case all Norah's letters and, of course, food we had or managed to get. It wouldn't push so we put two runners on the bottom, attached a piece of rope in front, enabling two of us to pull and the other two to push. We were a lot better off than some as we didn't have to carry everything on our backs.

We used to meet civilians from other villages sometimes on the roadside. The march was from Gleiwitz and we went over the mountains into Czechoslovakia and this was rather beautiful, with its pine trees and forests with heavy snow lying all around. Our chest slid along quite easily on its runners. The Czechoslovakian people were friendly and we sometimes managed to get into their houses and sit by the fire. Their kitchens seemed quite modern with up-to-date ranges. I remember passing a signpost – Prague 102 kilometres. Then on another occasion seeing a signpost to Dresden. We were still managing to camp in barns at night, occasionally having two or three days rest at a time. It was a long, cold and exhausting march and we were all weary not knowing where we were going and when it would end.

Once again the Red Cross miraculously found us and came to our rescue. I remember on one occasion during the march, seeing a white coach with a red cross on the side of it arriving at one of the farms. We were issued with the precious 10 lb (approx. 5 kilos), Red Cross parcels. It was a real treat and of course helped once again to boost morale and we were able to share out the food amongst us.

We also saw some Auschwitz prisoners being force-marched, dressed in their distinct striped pyjama-like uniforms. They were in a terrible condition and were crawling along the road. Quite frequently we would witness one collapsing in the snow by the roadside and being dragged across the road and shot in front of us by one of the German guards and their bodies just left lying where they had been shot. Terrible!

We saw Russian prisoners being similarly treated. They did not have the Geneva Convention to protect them. On different occasions we saw these poor souls being marched along in columns and if they weren't able to make it they were also shot.

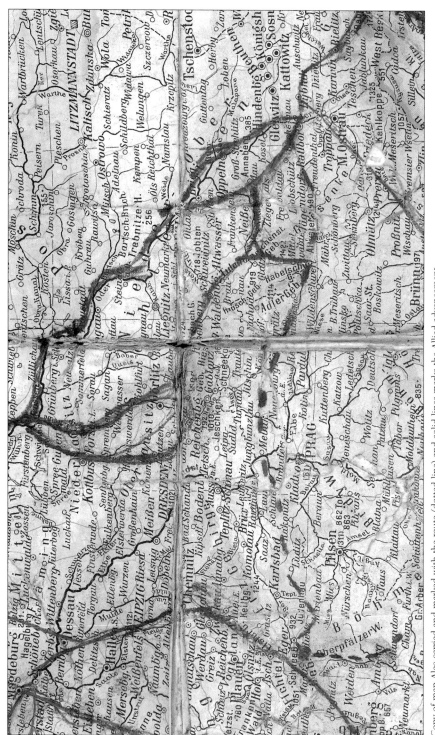

Copy of map Alec carried and marked with the route (dotted line) and solid lines marks the Allied advancement.

One of the lads whom I had known for a few years and had been in the same working party said to me, 'I can't make it.' He was very tired, had sore feet and was generally 'plum worn out'. Fortunately, they informed him that he was going to be left behind and that he would probably fall into the hands of the Russians. I quickly wrote a letter to my father telling him I was all right. I asked him if he would post the letter once he got back home. He was taken by the Russians and evacuated from Odessa on the Black Sea and he miraculously got home to Liverpool before me and sent the letter to my father. It was quite remarkable really; I didn't think he would have been treated so well.

George Hemsworth didn't smoke, so we always had his cigarettes to barter with. We were marching along one day and used some to barter with a civilian and ended up buying a pony on the march! We only had it for a short time and used it for towing our chest.

We marched to the very end of Czechoslovakia then out into Bavaria – I remember a baden – which was a spa, Villesbaden. We seemed to strike south. It was now the middle of March and the beginning of spring and the snow was melting on the road. The sun was getting stronger and our sledge was harder to pull as it was still on runners. We managed to overcome this problem by buying a pram from a civilian and having taken the wheels off, attached them to the bottom of our box. This was fine, until our commandant was changed and the new one issued orders that everything had to be carried on our backs and prams etc had to be discarded. So that was the end of our chest and we had to carry what we could on our shoulders in knapsacks. Sadly, I had to discard all of Norah's letters, they had to go, but I kept her photograph.

We did see quite a lot of air activity by the Americans and one day when they saw our column they thought at first we were Germans and did start to strafe and bomb us. Fortunately, we formed a cross on the ground to inform them that we were friends. We were lucky and we did not bear any casualties.

It was now the 24th April, 1945 and we were still striking south. The weather was getting warmer and we had just arrived on a big farm in Bavaria. I was busy cooking some stolen spuds and we had a tin of beef. Word arrived that tanks had been seen in the distance, we dropped everything and ran across the fields to meet American tanks. They were part of General Patton's Army that had broken through – 'Blood and Guts Patton' as he was affectionately known. The soldiers said, 'Hey guys help yourselves you are free! Now you are in charge of the guards!' They gave us some rifles. We quickly went back to camp and took our guards prisoner and handed them over to the Yanks!

JANUAR FEBRUAR MÄRZ APRIL MAI JUNI

1945

George Hemsworth's calendar that he kept showing the route taken on the march

The first thing we did after that was go and kill a deer we had seen earlier in the wood, got it back to the farm, skinned it, hung it up and then cooked it. Schwandorf was the nearest village and we made a beeline for it but found empty shops – the Americans had beaten us to it but we still managed to get a little food and liquid refreshment.

By a strange coincidence this was the day that the Daily Mail newspaper carried the headline – 'All PoWs to 'Stay Put!' – Germans agree.

Next day we watched our German guards being marched away. This was freedom at last after five years – what joy! I remember all the large American vehicles with big black men driving them – it was a lovely sight.

After about three days we were collected together in groups and taken in large Yank vehicles to the nearest aerodrome in Regensberg. Sitting on the tarmac were Dakotas – these aircrafts had been passenger planes at one time and had been stripped out and used to supply Patton's advance army with petrol. We thought that these would then be used to ferry us back to Britain and the white cliffs of Dover that we had been so looking forward to seeing after all these years! No, we didn't go there, but they flew us to Reims in France. Crossing over Germany I looked out of the plane and I have never seen such devastation, everywhere you looked there were damaged and bombed buildings in villages, towns and cities.

Dakota in the 1960s.

We landed in Reims and were taken to the American camp and we had delicious buffet canteen food, where you helped yourself. Our eyes lit up at the sight of scrambled eggs and bacon, white bread, milk - something we had not seen for five years. It was just so good and knowing also that we would be shipped back to England before long.

It was VE Day (Victory in Europe Day) and there were great celebrations in the city and there were wonderful joyous parties in the streets. George and I decided to climb up the tower inside the Cathedral and look out from the top where we saw all the crowds of people enjoying themselves – it was great! When we came down we found the door locked, so we had to climb up again and attract somebody's attention so that we would be let out. There was great joy from the French crowd to the British PoWs.

The following day we had to have a medical examination. First thing I said to the American was, 'Oh we are lousy, we have been for five years.' 'Come here Guys,' he said. They got out some powder, shook it down the back of our necks, down our shirts and down the front. That was DDT – we never had any more lice after that. The Germans didn't have DDT, they didn't know what it was.

They found I had impetigo on my head. I had caught this with living in dirty barns and other such places. The doctor told me, 'You will not be able to go home yet, as you will have to go into hospital.' I was in for ten days and lived on the most wonderful food and had all the very best treatment. The joy of having white sheets on the bed! I was given light/heat (infra-red) treatment and eventually cured and passed the medical and went out to the aerodrome once again. I had to wait for a couple of days for transport and travelled home in a Lancaster bomber that had been stripped out – there were fifteen PoWs per plane.

We came in and landed near Whipsnade Zoo on the outskirts of London and I remember looking out over the bomb bay and seeing the white cliffs of Dover. I rang my father and caught the 10 pm mail train from Euston and arrived at Lancaster about 5 am. My father met me at the station and took me home and back to 'Civvy Street'.

Before I leave this important chapter in my life I would like to emphasise what an appalling time we had and the dreadful conditions we had to endure. I cannot remember all that happened and the terrible sights we saw. During this enforced march I carried a map with me and the dotted line is the route we took and the solid pen marked routes are those kept of the advancing Allied Armies as received on my crystal wireless set from

'Voice of America'. The map is well worn and backed in strong paper. George Hemsworth also wrote on a calendar the route taken although many of the old place names have changed since the war. The transcript of George's calendar is put in the appendix for anyone wanting to trace the route.

The Germans did not really know what to do with we prisoners, how to feed us or where to put us at night. Near the end of the march, they sometimes got us up in the early hours and moved us further on. Other times they told us we were moving, got us ready and were sometimes some hours before we actually moved off – it just got more and more chaotic as the Germans were becoming increasingly aware that they were gradually losing the war!

The march that we took part in lasted for nearly three months. I am not sure of the distance we walked/marched it is difficult to judge but estimate it to be around a thousand miles. As to the reason for the march – it is my opinion that it was not only to get us away from the Russians but to take us into Bavaria, as Berchtesgaden was thought to be going to be the hideout of Hitler and his girlfriend Eva Braun, a fortified area in the mountains – with his cronies Goering and Goebbles etc – and to use us as hostages. This again is only an opinion – the outcome of course is history!

Norah in ATS uniform.

Chapter Eleven

Home on Leave and Norah

I was now home on leave for six weeks and very much looking forward to seeing Norah and taking up from where we had left off if possible. She had written to me all the time I was a PoW and her letters had meant so much to me as well as the thought of getting home and seeing her again.

Norah was still in the army and was a sergeant mechanic stationed at Quernmore Park, Caton, in the Army Camp there. She had been four years in the Auxiliary Territorial Service (ATS) the women's branch of the army. This was a collecting and distribution station for different types of vehicles that came directly from the manufacturers and then distributed to the different units all over the country. Other vehicles were in for minor repairs or stored there until required.

It was great seeing her again and I thought lets get away together. So I said to her, 'Let's go away for the weekend and stay at a nice hotel?' She must have mentioned it to her mother and she wrote to us both saying, 'I think you should wait until you are married. I don't think you should take the gilt off the gingerbread!' What's more we didn't!

In those six weeks that I was at home I was fortunate enough to have Norah and she helped to counsel me for I was completely lost – traumatised. I was shy, didn't like meeting people and I did not understand what they were saying or talking about. I was also very worried, had no confidence in myself or in my abilities. I didn't have any trade or qualifications and I didn't know what I was going to do. All I knew was that I wanted to get married. I knew if I was married I wanted to keep my wife properly, there was no dole or national assistance then. When a man married it was his intention to keep the house and his family. So I went through a very worrying period of time. Nowadays we would have received counselling to help us get over what we had been through but it didn't exist then. Thankfully I had Norah and it was she who got me through and back on my feet again.

At the end of my leave I was 'called-up' again to attend a basic training camp at Hartford Bridge, near Morpeth. We did our basic training, which was full pack and rifle, and were given the full treatment in preparation for sending us out to Japan or the Far East, as we were still not demobbed. The training lasted for about a month.

Armoured vehicle being checked out by Norah and sprayed.

Norah busy working (in leather sleeveless jacket) – note the vehicles parked ready to go out.

Norah (2nd from right on back row) with Barbara (her sister)
next to her at Quernmore Park, relaxing with other girls.

We used to go into Newcastle for the evening and one evening I met my old friend and buddy Jim McCabe (PoW) in a bar. He was now stationed in Newcastle. We had such a reunion that I came back to camp on the milk wagon in the early hours of the following morning!

The Atomic Bomb was dropped in the Far East and, of course, the war with Japan was now over. This was great news and that was the end of the war for me and I got an early demob on 11th August, 1945. I went down to York and got my discharge papers (effective date being 28th November, 1945) and we were given our discharge clothing. This consisted of a trilby hat, mackintosh and a grey suit, with a white stripe and that was our 'demob issue'. I then thankfully went home. I received the 1939/43 Star Medal and my military conduct was stated as 'very good'.

But before moving on I must round things off here. What happened to the rest of the Regiment after we got captured? I later found out that they were successfully evacuated from Dunkirk with thousands of others. After this they were sent to Singapore and were unfortunately captured by the Japanese. They were treated very badly as PoWs and many died or returned in a very bad condition.

Richard Swainson (solicitor) and Captain of D' Troop was in a Japanese PoW Camp – he recovered and returned to his family business and died aged 85.

Donald Wadell, a clerk in the Battery Office, was evacuated from Dunkirk and was commissioned. He later became Lancaster City Town Clerk (Chief Executive) and is now retired and still lives in Lancaster. Also working in the Battery Office was Ken Dowbiggen, prior to this he worked at Storeys of Lancaster. He was evacuated from Dunkirk, served in Singapore and was later captured by the Japanese. After being released and enjoying a period of recuperation, he returned to Storeys.

Tony Birkbeck was evacuated from Dunkirk and spent the rest of the war in Burma. We met up afterwards and spent many happy days with his brother Maurice (Captain) together. He had been captured with me and put in a separate camp for commissioned officers called an Oflag, for five years. (Non-commissioned officers were put into Stalags). Sadly both brothers died in their fifties. I am godfather to Mark, Maurice's eldest son who now runs a very successful business – 'The House of Bruar' in Blair Athol. He began the Lakeland Sheepskin Shops, which he sold and started the Jumpers business at Cowan Bridge, near Kirkby Lonsdale, which he also sold before going to Blair Athol.

As to my three good friends, George, Jim and Gilbert who undoubtedly helped me get through those terrible years and whom I will never forget. What became of them? George eventually came out of the army and went into business. He sadly died a few years ago and his widow is now living in Poole, Dorset. Jim McCabe emigrated to Canada and sadly died seven or eight years ago. Gilbert I sadly lost touch with.

Chapter Twelve

Normality – Family and Farming

Back in Lancaster, I was staying with father now a widower living on his own. I said to him, 'Father are you getting married again?' He said, 'No, I am not, I am having housekeepers, I can get rid of them if I don't like them!' So that was father!

My father was still doing a small amount of supplying cattle to East Anglia, buying mainly from auction marts and a few from friends and family he had always dealt with. He thought there was an opening for me to come in and help him and to take on the business and enlarge it as he had done.

Meanwhile Norah and I married on the 2nd March, 1946 at St. Paul's Church, Scotforth, Lancaster. The reception was at her parents' house, Temple Villa. My brother was best man and her sister Barbara was bridesmaid. We had our honeymoon in Torquay. We had a night at the Red Lion in Shrewsbury. Next day we lunched with Sid Barker (my uncle) the owner of the Royal Hotel, Symonds Yat, Ross-on-Wye. We returned home to live at 7 Morecambe Road, Morecambe.

The following year we had a holiday to Montreux on the Orient Express for ten days. We skied at the Roche de Naye and returned home by train via Lille where we stayed with the Wacheux family for a week. We had great celebrations and opened some 1939 bottled Bass!

I helped my father for a year or so but I could see there was not a lot of future in dealing. I had perhaps not the same gift that he had for trading, so consequently I thought I would like to farm. I had very little knowledge of farming and only an outside view, I had never taken part in any practical work. That was my intention and so I attempted to

Alec and Norah on their wedding day on the 2nd March, 1946.

Norah and Alec saying goodbye to Jackie and Paulette Wacheux at Lille in 1947.

The square in Gondecourt in the late 1960/70s. On the left are the cinema and church.

buy a farm first of all. I had my sights set on Low Hyning Farm (just off the A6, approximately two miles north of Carnforth) but that was bought by Lord Peel's agent old Dick Turner who had already bought the mansion, Low Hyning House, and naturally wanted the farm to go with it.

Through people we knew, we ascertained that Lord Peel didn't require the farm but would let it to me for three years under a gentleman's agreement and I would leave it at the end of the term. I realised I needed help on the farm and remembered Jack Johnson, auctioneer and friend in the Lune Valley, telling me at the market one day that his farm man had a brother wanting a job.

So when I rented the farm from Lord Peel, the first thing I did was to find this Bill Gibson who was working on a farm - Murley Moss, Kendal and arrange for him to come to Low Hyning. I took up farming on the 12th April 1948, I remember that date well, as it was the day our daughter, Angela, was born in the nursing home at the top of Cannon Hill, in Lancaster.

I travelled backwards and forwards every day to Low Hyning as I was still living in Morecambe. We made good progress the first year. I started with one hundred and sixty acres which wasn't licensed as a TB free holding but I cleaned up all the buildings, the land was rested and I was granted a licence which meant I could purchase TB attested cattle. At that time cattle tested clear of TB were sold in a different market to those which had failed and were known as reactors. I decided to buy twenty TB clear Shorthorn milking cows, ten in calf cows and heifers, thirty Masham ewes and a Suffolk tup which arrived in the guards van of a train from Ipswich.

I bought a milking machine powered by a small petrol engine, quite a new one, a 'Simplex' from a Penrith firm. There was no electricity or water at Low Hyning. We had a ram that supplied water to one or two big troughs in the yard and also to one of the top fields. The rest of the land was without water. I managed to buy an ex-army generator and produced electricity for the farmhouse where Mr Gibson and his wife lived. Being TB tested we had to have a steriliser to sterilise all the equipment after each milking, so I bought a steam boiler for this purpose. We were milking twice a day and I travelled daily from Morecambe Road to the farm setting off at 6.30 am and returning home at 7 pm. We had six acres of turnips and two acres of mangolds which were stored for winter feed. These had to be thinned out as seedlings by hand, crawling on your knees with bags tied round them – and I did that as well. We also had half an acre of kale and an acre of potatoes. The potatoes had to be planted by hand, rows ridged up, filled with muck forked off a trailer. Then we carried the swill (basket

Alec in the driver's seat of the ex-army lorry the Wacheux family used for delivering wine whilst on his visit with them in 1947.

made from willow or oak) with potatoes in – dropped a seed every foot (30 cm) to eighteen inches (46 cm). These stitches (rows) had to be split, kept clean, knocked down, broken down and rowed up again with a harrow. We had an awful field that year it was full of couch grass (known locally as wicks or twitch) but still managed to get a reasonable crop.

Then of course they had to be lifted when ready, they were picked by hand, into swills or buckets and put into hundredweight hessian bags. They were taken into the barn to be stored and sorted out during the wintertime. Anything diseased, chipped or rotten was taken out and the small ones we used as seed for the following year. The rest were bagged up for sale. All this sorting out was done on the floor on your knees. The potatoes bagged for sale were taken to the wholesaler, Sowdens in Lancaster and some we kept for ourselves or sold to people in the village. I used to deliver the orders in the village. Sometimes they would maybe say to me, 'We are going to store them all winter, could you take them upstairs and put them on that spare bedroom floor?' Quite a weight I had to struggle with. Nowadays they have half hundredweights – much more sense!

We wanted all the revenue we could get so we kept a few hens and I thought we ought to have a few goslings for Christmas and a few turkeys. I went to the village blacksmiths, McGaffigans, in Bolton-le-Sands, to buy twenty goslings and nursed them in a shed with a lamp for heat, fed them through the summer with a bit of grass and corn towards the end. A week or two before Christmas they had to be starved first and then plucked by hand. I had never plucked a goose before and don't think I ever will again, if I can help it! Worst job I ever had to do with two or three people helping. We hung them for a week, drew them (cleaned out the innards), packed them and took them round to the people who had ordered them. Lord Peel was altering the buildings and the house and we got orders from the workmen and had to deliver them round different parts of Lancaster.

We were making good progress and went to the agent at Davis & Bowring. I asked, 'What are your intentions? Am I still required to leave at the end of three years?' They made enquiries and said, 'Yes, they wanted the farm and I would have to leave it.' Lord Peel had already bought Warton Grange, another farm, as a wedding present for his wife in Warton village, but went on to say that I could rent that farm and could move in right away if I wished and he would move to Low Hyning. That is what we did. We moved in February 1949 – his cows went up the main street and mine came down the back lane!

Progress was made with many difficulties. I remember buying a lot of the machinery with my army savings and with help from my, now, very elderly

Bill Gibson in 1948.

Low Hyning Farmhouse and buildings in 1948.

father. I bought a grey Fergie (Ferguson) tractor and tip-up trailer from the Massey Ferguson agent, Hoggarths, in Sandes Avenue, Kendal. That was quite revolutionary then, together with a ridging plough and some harrows, and had them delivered. That was really modernising, only a few people had tractors then and were just beginning to get rid of their horses. We were still making hay in the same old-fashioned way, which was carting it, loose and mooing (storing) it in the barns. Machinery bought in those days was of course the old horse machinery and once you were sitting behind a tractor there were numerous troubles and breakdowns much to our frustration! We soon overcame them and forgot the hard times.

Things were not so easy as they are today by any means. Later on I developed quite a poultry unit at Warton Grange, I got an old shed or two, built up some huts and had at one time a one thousand hens in deep litter and some in batteries. The eggs used to go to the Egg Marketing Board to their egg-packing stations. They all had to be washed, cleaned and counted into large crates, two hundred and forty eggs in a box. These were taken into Lancaster (Quay) and each egg would be graded and stamped with a lion thereon!

The poultry were mostly on 'deep litter'. That meant the hut had sawdust on the floor, perches and nest boxes. There were hoppers of food suspended from the ceiling, with grit and water. When the old hens had finished their laying life, they would be killed and plucked by a plucking machine – there was quite a sale for old boilers – dressed and we retailed them as best we could.

We also had quite a lot of wild cats running round the farm that used to breed quite frequently. We bought turkey eggs and hatched them off under

Wilkinson's Butchers Shop window in Lancaster with our turkeys dressed and ready for sale!

Aerial view of Warton Grange Farm – middle of picture

Norah with Paul and Angela in the garden at Inglebank in 1953

hens. We put the chicks in a shed and one of the cats got in and destroyed quite a lot. I went along to the RSPCA and told them that I had got some wild cats about the farm and they supplied me with a cat trap and some chloroform. We trapped those cats and put them in a sack with some chloroform and disposed of them that way. It was all quite legal in those days.

Next Christmas, we had turkeys again as they were quite a nice revenue. The difficulty was always getting just the right size for the customer, as they all wanted a small hen and, unfortunately, they didn't all come that way. There were always some large cocks to find a home for as well. It was fairly successful, but we lost quite a few from a disease called, Gapes, which they got from picking up worms from the grass. To avoid this we put them on a veranda. I bought one that held thirty; it was off the ground, had a wire floor and surround, with covered roof and trough outside. A young lad, the local joiner's apprentice, built me another one the following year. It was big enough for a hundred turkeys and by now we had bought a dry plucking machine, so there were no more problems with Gapes or plucking!

We had kept dairy and sheep at Warton Grange. We eventually disbanded sheep apart from buying store lambs in the autumn from the fells of Cumberland and leaving them on the grass to follow the cows during the winter. We sold them as strong hogs in the spring.

In the 1960s, with the aid of a Government grant, we drained a large 30-acre field that we called 'Myers'. This was near the farm buildings and was noted for flooding during periods of heavy rainfall and high tides. The field is below sea level and also forms a catchments area for water coming off Warton Crag. A complicated drainage scheme was drawn up by the Ministry of Agriculture and Fisheries and was supervised by Mr Baxter (Drainage Officer), the field was drained, 30,000 tiles were laid and the water was drained into a sump and lifted by a submersible pump to the outfall of the River Keer where there was a sluice gate. This proved to be very successful, though still floods occasionally in the middle at high tide and times of heavy rainfall.

During the war years, farmers were required to produce as much as possible to support the country – due to the great shortage caused by the many convoys sunk in the Atlantic. A lot of food was still rationed until 1947-8 and farmers were required to continue to produce as much food as possible and this would also help the country's Balance of Payments. In return, we received aid and support from the Government and we, of course, took full advantage of it. During the years I have expanded and modernised the

Grey Fergie (TVO – tractor vaporising oil) like the one Alec used to have

Early silage vehicles – tractors, silage trailers and Kidds silage blower in 'Prairie Field', Warton Grange Farm in the 1970s.

buildings and equipment. I have taken advice from the Ministry of Agriculture and Fisheries (now Department for Environment, Food and Rural Affairs – DEFRA) together with advice from ICI (Imperial Chemical Industries) and BOCM (British Oil and Cake Mills) and other advisory people. Our farms are still ongoing but with falling returns, as we do not always receive a fair price for our produce mainly due to imports and lack of Government intervention.

We had originally started with a dairy herd of twenty at Low Hyning and we now have in the vicinity of two hundred plus milkers. In 1963 we obtained Hillam House Farm at Cockerham – it was one hundred and thirty acres. It was tenanted to begin with and when the tenant died we got vacant possession in 1965. I split the land into three lots and grass let it to three neighbours, Henry Birkett, Brian Lawson and Henry Lawson. These three farmers would willingly give it up if and when I wanted it. This was to give me time to improve the house and farm buildings that were run down. After a few years I gradually took back all the land and farmed it for a short period.

Building a slurry pit at Hillam Houses Farm in the early 1970s. Beef cubicles to the left, old shippon and farmhouse. On the left is Bill Wilkinson and Maurice Burrow.

I farmed Warton Grange for nearly fifty years. When we sold our Morecambe Road house, I bought a house in the middle of Warton, called 'The Cedars' to enable me to be near the farm. Later, another house, 'Inglebank', came up for sale in the village and this caught Norah's eye, so we bought it in 1952 and spent many happy years there.

My son, Michael, was born on the 23rd January, 1951 and this completed our family. I was still helping my father who was still going to the auction marts, so I was going down to Ipswich as well and this continued until 1960.

I took father to the last sale in November 1960, the Luke Fair in Kirkby Stephen. He said, 'This is the 60th time I've been here!' He always enjoyed them and of course he had been to sixty sales and bought cattle there – which was rather a long time. My father died in 1963, aged eighty-six.

Norah's father had a successful family butcher's shop at No 8 Market Street, Lancaster. His father who had also been a butcher, had a butcher's shop in Cheapside, Lancaster, which is now a Bank. When he retired, his son Tom moved the business to Market Street around the beginning of the First World War. His cousin, who had fought in the Dardenelles (in the straights on the approach to Istanbul and the entrance to the Black Sea) joined him in the business after being demobbed and was made manager.

Tom had a staff of eleven and used to call them his 'football team'! Tom bought all his cattle, sheep and pigs locally from farms or the Auction Mart, in Thurnham Street, Lancaster. (New Auction Mart is now on Wyresdale Road, Golgotha, Lancaster). Either he or his men slaughtered them at the slaughterhouse, near the Auction Mart. During the winter months from January-April/May he went further north where the cattle were fattened in yards (sheds). He bought his Aberdeen Angus beef from Fraser's Auction Mart, Perth and was renowned for its quality.

When Tom, my father-in-law, decided to retire in the early 1950s he offered the business to me to run in conjunction with the rest of his family – Harry Banks-Lyon who had married his other daughter, Barbara, and my wife, Norah. I was the buyer and business manager and Harry Banks-Lyon looked after the accounts.

I continued in much the same way buying locally from farmers and at the Auction Mart in Lancaster. During the winter months, off-season I travelled to Bishop Auckland and would buy a fortnight's supply of cattle and sheep, which we kept on our Warton Grange farm prior to slaughtering. For beef I would buy Aberdeen Angus, Charolais and Limousin Cross. I would buy Masham and Suffolk Cross sheep. We would use a couple of porker pigs a week. I had some good staff: - William Orange (manager); Frank Westby, Catherine Rankin, Catherine Baxter (Overtown) and Bob.

After sixteen years we decided to sell the butchers business in Lancaster and concentrate on the two farms as these were changing times in agriculture and a lot of foresight and work was required.

Harry Banks-Lyon's father, also called Harry, had started the shoe shop in Church Street, Lancaster. Harry helped his dad in his business after being demobbed, after the war and continued running the business until he died in March 2002. This business (Banks-Lyon Shoes) is now carried on by his son Jonathan. His other son, Rodney has a successful jeweller's shop next door (Banks-Lyon Jewellers).

Angela, our daughter, went to St. Anne's School, Windermere as a boarder. On her first day we decided to stop and have a coffee at a café in Windermere, where we happened to meet Norman and Elizabeth Manners and their daughter Ruth, from Fawcett Valley, Aldbrough St. John, Richmond who was also going to St. Anne's School. That was the start of our friendship with the Manners family and the girls and parents have remained close friends ever since.

On leaving school Angela went into nursing at the Royal Southern Hospital in Liverpool. She qualified as an SRN and worked in the Orthopaedic Ward at the Royal Lancaster Infirmary.

My son Michael was then at Myerscough Agricultural College doing his HND in Agriculture and wished to do a six months' practical course. I asked Norman Manners if he would take him on at his arable farm. He said he did not take students, but his cousin William Manners of Thornton Hall, near Piercebridge, Darlington might possibly. An interview was arranged and he was accepted and Michael successfully completed his course. Whilst there on the farm he met Elizabeth, their daughter and they started going out together and later married. They naturally moved into Hillam House Farm and joined me in the business. Michael farmed that as his own and as we had a beef unit I sent our own beef calves from the dairy herd at Warton Grange to him. He then wanted to use the experience he had gained in rearing pigs, while working on the Manners family farm, and consequently he wanted to keep pigs. He set up a pig breeding and finishing unit that he is still successfully running today with large White X Landrace.

Paul Barker, (Alec's grandson) aged two, standing next to the Massey Ferguson tractor at Hillam House Farm in 1980.

George Hemsworth and Alec at Inglebank, Warton in the early 1960s.

Maurice Burrow; Paul (Alec's grandson); Alan Shuttleworth; Bryan Galloway
and 'Cindy' the black Labrador, at Warton Grange Farm in 2000.

Chapter Thirteen

Retirement

I've been going to Tenerife for twenty years now. When I first went there I had occasion to meet Bob Earl, a farmer, who originally came from Wigton, in Cumbria and had moved to the Lincolnshire area of Newark. He rented a farm there to begin with which he later bought and added to and was then farming a thousand acres. He said to me, 'I remember your father, he used to come into Wigton Auction Mart and buy cattle there when I was a boy and my father was selling.' That, of course, was Hope's Auction Mart. It is a small world!

Hilda, my sister, died in 1980, she and Charles had one child, Tony, who was a doctor but is now retired. Owen, my brother, sadly died two years later in 1982. He had married Ruth Parker, nee Geary, but they did not have any children. Owen had a stepson, John Parker, Ruth's son from her first husband. John is now retired from being a vet and in 2005 he was made president of the Royal Veterinary Society of Great Britain. Owen was very fond of grouse shooting. He was an officer, in the Royal Artillery during the Second World War and was in charge of an anti-aircraft battery in Norfolk and also in Orkney. He was once asked whether they had shot down any aircraft. 'Only one, unfortunately one of ours!'

Angela married Robert Hughes on 20th February, 1971 at St Oswald's Church, Warton. Robert Hughes is a property developer, they met when he was a surveyor in Lancaster and lived at Aldcliffe just behind the hospital where Angela worked. They have three children, a boy and two girls, all now grown up. Roger went to Lancaster Grammar School and then to University in Nottingham and works with his father in his development business. Janette and Kate went to The Lakes School, Windermere. Kate has a degree in design and Janette in photography. Janette has now a successful business in wedding photography and Kate is teaching in Sheffield. Angela stopped working when she had her family. When they moved to Windermere and the children were grown up, she took up a position as school nurse at St. Anne's, her old school. She remained there for twenty-five years. By great coincidence, the school sold off part of the building called Chapel Ridding which Robert bought and developed. They now live in part of the house.

Michael and Elizabeth have two grown-up children. Paul and Andrew both went to Sedbergh School and then to Harper Adams Agricultural College in Shropshire. Paul is now farming Warton Grange Farm in partnership with

Family gathering at the Merewood Hotel, Windermere in 1998 – a joint celebration, Alec and Norah's Golden Wedding and Angela and Robert's Silver Wedding. Back row l to r: Robert, Angela, Janette, Kate and Roger Hughes; Paul, Andrew, Liz and Michael Barker. Alec and Norah sitting down.

Michael who is still running his pig unit at Hillam House Farm, Cockerham. Andrew qualified as a surveyor and valuer and worked for a time at Cluttons in Kent and Oxford. He is now in partnership in his own business in Ashford and Oxford.

Michael diversified from farming twelve years ago and together with Elizabeth and a neighbouring farmer, Richard Halhead, bought a disused petrol station on the A65 just outside Ingleton, on the busy main road between the Yorkshire Dales and the Lake District. With the help of Mark Birkbeck, they had the foresight to build a farm shop which they stocked with locally sourced country produce and aptly called it 'Country Harvest' it has become a successful, thriving business.

When Michael came into the business he took over the farm and I gradually withdrew from it. Occasionally he would give me little jobs to do and he would maybe ring up and say, 'I would like you to take some cattle to the auction Dad' which I was delighted in doing or he would maybe say, 'I would like two hundred sheep from Kendal to put on the farm.'

I retired from it finally six years ago when I moved here to Berners Close, Grange-Over-Sands. I am still always interested in what is going on and occasionally I am asked advice on something or where was this drain or where was that? There are two hundred acres now, with a dairy herd of two hundred plus, Holstein Friesians. During the years we have had some jolly good staff at Warton Grange. Bill Gibson who worked for me for eighteen years before retiring and moving into a house in Warton, with his wife Madge. They are both now sadly dead. For thirty-five years we had Alan Shuttleworth doing the milking and general farm work and Maurice Burrow doing tractor work for nearly forty years and he is still helping Paul.

The property I live in was a large house converted into luxury flats by my son-in-law, Robert, and has beautiful views over the estuary towards Morecambe Bay and enjoys the fine weather from the Gulf Stream. We bought our own place in Tenerife nineteen years ago. Norah had gone there with her parents in 1929 on holiday and I had also holidayed there. We rented an apartment for a year or two to begin with and eventually we bought one at Las Gigantes. We still have the same property which all the family have enjoyed thoroughly and used – all the children have been. We have had many other holidays. Norah and I have gone round the world, to the Caribbean and the Mediterranean cruising and enjoyed river holidays in Europe and Tenerife.

In 2003 three of our grandchildren married. Janette married Bernard Marshall at the Windermere Royal Yacht Club; Kate married Adam Jackson at the Motor Boat Club; and Paul married Helen Rosendale at the Grange Hotel, in Grange-over-Sands. Robert Hughes has just finished his two years as Commodore at the Royal Windermere Yacht Club and greeted Princess Anne when she visited the Club this year being their centenary year.

Sadly, Norah passed away twelve months ago. She developed a lung infection and did not react to antibiotics and died on the 24th April, 2004 after fifty-eight happy years of marriage. My son, daughter and partners have been a tremendous help and I have spent a lot of time with them and it has helped me a lot. I have managed to fare on my own completely and went to Tenerife last winter where I have many friends who helped me and made it easy. Though, as everyone knows who has lost someone dear, it is never easy – every time one opens a drawer there is something there that brings memories flooding back.

I keep myself busy as I have many hobbies - gardening, doing jobs, socialising, fine wine, DIY – carpentry, furnishing, picture framing and I have my own work bench in the garage. I am fortunate in having Jack Webster, known as 'Yorkie' (ex-miner) from Carnforth, who comes occasionally to help me with the garden and is now a good friend. Two years ago our garden received first prize in the 'Grange in Bloom' competition in the section, 'Garden seen from the road' and won the shield. This year we managed 'commended' and received a certificate from Grange Civic Society.

I have had a good life, made all the richer by my family and the friends I have made along the way. I hope you have enjoyed reading about my life and in doing so I have fulfilled my promise to my family in allowing my memoirs to be written.

Alec Barker

Appendix

This is the transcription of the route of the march from the calendar that George Hemsworth's kept in 1945. Set out below is the actual route taken. Some of the names have changed since the end of the war as a result of territories going back to Poland and Czechoslovakia etc. Alec's nephew, Tony Chaloner has added additional information which is in italics, to assist anybody trying to trace the route taken in today's map. Please note references on the calendar e.g. '160 Home' etc are the actual number of letters that George sent home to his family.

21st January		Sunday	Work
22nd	"	Monday	Move 10pm (*commencement of march*)
23rd	"	Tuesday	Klein Buchenau (*marched all day*)
24th	"	Wednesday	Lohnau (*crossed Oder midday*)
25th	"	Thursday	Wernersdorf (*Barewitz*)
26th	"	Friday	Day's Rest
27th	"	Saturday	Bransdorf *and Jagersdorf*
28th	"	Sunday	Day's Rest
29th	"	Monday	M. Kutzendorf
30th	"	Tuesday	Rest
31st	"	Wednesday	Deutsch Lodnitz
1st February	"	Thursday	Kronersdorf
2nd	"	Friday	Day's Rest
3rd	"	Saturday	Hliwitz (*Glimitz Elfriede*)
4th	"	Sunday	Day's Rest
5th	"	Monday	Alt Meletein
6th	"	Tuesday	Rest
7th	"	Wednesday	Alt Stadt
8th	"	Thursday	Nikl
9-12th	"	Fri-Monday	Rest
13th	"	Tuesday	Osik Czecho. S (*crossed Czech border to Leitomichl to Osik*)
14th	"	Wednesday	Hermannitz
15th	"	Thursday	Oberjellen (*Clotzeu to*)
16th	"	Friday	Rest
17th	"	Saturday	Hoch Chworne (*difficult to read*) – *Jarrow* Holitz)
18th	"	Sunday	Wischka on Elbe (*Koniggratz – passed sign 102 km to Prague, Dresden 227 km*)
19th	"	Monday	Rest
20th	"	Tuesday	Leipe
21st	"	Wednesday	Obergut Wasser (*Gutwasser*)
22nd	"	Thursday	Rest (*Luschan just off the main road to Deisen*)
23rd	"	Friday	Luschan
24th	"	Saturday	Libun
25th	"	Sunday	Rest (*Garbolka 165 km Dresden – Jungbaulow Vienna 295 km, Prague 50 km*)

26th	"	Monday	Oberbausow
27th	"	Tuesday	Kropatsch
28th	"	Wednesday	Wrutitz – Rest
1st March	"	Thursday	Oberschistwi (24 km march. Crossed Elbe 28 km Prague)
2nd	"	Friday	Bukot (Buklot?)
3rd	"	Saturday	Rest
4th	"	Sunday	Schischitz (Kraluh Schischitz)
5th	"	Monday	Jedomielitz (Karlsbad Rd)
6th	"	Tuesday	Rest
7th	"	Wednesday	Okraschau (Kraschau, crossed border in Sudetenland)
8th	"	Thursday	S. Holleschowitz
9th	"	Friday	Rest
10th	"	Saturday	Rest
11th	"	Sunday	Liebkowitz
12th	"	Monday	Rest
13th	"	Tuesday	Bohentsch (13 km to Karlsbad)
14th	"	Wednesday	Otrossau (Frossan)
15th	"	Thursday	Rest
16th	"	Friday	Einsiedl (valley of Petschau 21 km to Marienbad)
17th	"	Saturday	Untergraming (difficult to read)
18th	"	Sunday	Hohendorf?
19th	"	Monday	Untersandau (Marienbad)
20th	"	Tuesday	Rest
21st	"	Wednesday	Gemaag (difficult to read)
22nd	"	Thursday	Kondrau (Walasassor)
23-27th	"	Tuesday	Rest (Viondau or Yondau, Bavaria)
28th-3rd April		Thursday	(Kondau)
4-14th	"	Saturday	Wildenau
15th	"	Sunday	Alten Stadt?
16th	"	Monday	Bechtsrieth
17th	"	Tuesday	Tannesburg? (Clian)
18th	"	Wednesday	Nunzenried
19th	"	Thursday	Stamsried
20-22nd	"	Fri-Sun	Rest (saw concentration camp prisoners)
23rd	"	Monday	Scrroting
24th	"	Tuesday	Tauschendorf (Village Ene of Regensbourg, half way to Czech frontier)
25th	"	Wednesday	Freed

Flew out from Regensburg to Reims, then to UK